The

O. Henry

Short Story Collection

Volume One

O. Henry

Contents

The Gift *of* The Magi

ne dollar and eighty-seven cents. That was all. And sixty cents of it was in pennies. Pennies saved one and two at a time by bulldozing the grocer and the vegetable man and the butcher until one's cheeks burned with the silent imputation of parsimony that such close dealing implied. Three times Della counted it. One dollar and eighty-seven cents. And the next day would be Christmas.

There was clearly nothing to do but flop down on the shabby little couch and howl. So Della did it. Which instigates the moral reflection that life is made up of sobs, sniffles, and smiles, with sniffles predominating.

While the mistress of the home is gradually subsiding from the first stage to the second, take a look at the home. A furnished flat at $8 per week. It did not exactly beggar description, but it certainly had that word on the lookout for the mendicancy squad.

In the vestibule below was a letter-box into which no letter would go, and an electric button from which no mortal finger could coax a ring. Also appertaining thereunto was a card bearing the name "Mr. James Dillingham Young."

The "Dillingham" had been flung to the breeze during a former period of prosperity when its possessor was being paid $30 per week. Now, when the income was shrunk to $20, though, they were thinking seriously of contracting to a modest and unassuming D. But whenever Mr. James Dillingham Young came home and reached his flat above he was called "Jim" and greatly hugged by Mrs. James Dillingham Young, already introduced to you as Della. Which is all very good.

Della finished her cry and attended to her cheeks with the powder rag. She stood by the window and looked out dully at a gray cat walking a gray fence in a gray backyard. Tomorrow would be Christmas Day, and she had only $1.87 with which to buy Jim a present. She had been saving every penny she could for months, with this result. Twenty dollars a week doesn't go far. Expenses had been greater than she had calculated. They always are. Only $1.87 to buy a present for Jim. Her Jim. Many a happy hour she had spent planning for something nice for him. Something fine and rare and sterling– something just a little bit near to being worthy of the honor of being owned by Jim.

There was a pier-glass between the windows of the room. Perhaps you have seen a pierglass in an $8 flat. A very thin and very agile person may, by observing his reflection in a rapid sequence of longitudinal strips, obtain a fairly accurate conception of his looks. Della, being slender, had mastered the art.

Suddenly she whirled from the window and stood before the glass. Her eyes were shining brilliantly, but her face had lost its color within twenty seconds. Rapidly she pulled down her hair and let it fall to its full length.

Now, there were two possessions of the James Dillingham Youngs in which they both took a mighty pride. One was Jim's gold watch that had been his father's and his grandfather's. The other was Della's hair. Had the queen of Sheba lived in the flat across the airshaft, Della would have let her hair hang out the window someday to dry just to depreciate Her Majesty's jewels and gifts. Had King Solomon been the janitor, with all his treasures piled up in the basement, Jim would have pulled out his watch every time he passed, just to see him pluck at his beard from envy.

So now Della's beautiful hair fell about her rippling and shining like a cascade of brown waters. It reached below her knee and made itself almost a garment for her. And then she did it up again nervously and quickly. Once she faltered for a minute and stood still while a tear or two splashed on the worn red carpet.

On went her old brown jacket; on went her old brown hat. With a whirl of skirts and with the brilliant sparkle still in her eyes, she fluttered out the door and down the stairs to the street.

Where she stopped the sign read: "Mme. Sofronie. Hair Goods of All Kinds." One flight up Della ran, and collected herself, panting. Madame, large, too white, chilly, hardly looked the "Sofronie."

"Will you buy my hair?" asked Della.

"I buy hair," said Madame. "Take yer hat off and let's have a sight at the looks of it."

Down rippled the brown cascade.

"Twenty dollars," said Madame, lifting the mass with a practiced hand.

"Give it to me quick," said Della.

Oh, and the next two hours tripped by on rosy wings. Forget the hashed metaphor. She was ransacking the stores for Jim's present.

She found it at last. It surely had been made for Jim and no one else. There was no other like it in any of the stores, and she had turned all of them inside out. It was a platinum fob chain simple and chaste in design, properly proclaiming its value by substance alone and not by meretricious ornamentation—as all good things should do. It was even worthy of The Watch. As soon as she saw it she knew that it must be Jim's. It was like him. Quietness and value—the description applied to both. Twenty-one dollars they took from her for it, and she hurried home with the 87 cents. With that chain on his watch Jim might be properly anxious about the time in any company. Grand as the watch was, he sometimes looked at it on the sly on account of the old leather strap that he used in place of a chain.

When Della reached home her intoxication gave way a little to prudence and reason. She got out her curling irons and lighted the gas and went to work repairing the ravages made by generosity added to love. Which is always a tremendous task, dear friends—a mammoth task.

Within forty minutes her head was covered with tiny, close-lying curls that made her look wonderfully like a truant schoolboy. She looked at her reflection in the mirror long, carefully, and critically.

"If Jim doesn't kill me," she said to herself, "before he takes a second look at me, he'll say I look like a Coney Island chorus girl. But what could I do—oh! what could I do with a dollar and eighty-seven cents?"

At 7 o'clock the coffee was made and the frying-pan was on the back of the stove hot and ready to cook the chops.

Jim was never late. Della doubled the fob chain in her hand and sat on the corner of the table near the door that he always entered. Then she heard his step on the stair

6

away down on the first flight, and she turned white for just a moment. She had a habit of saying a little silent prayer about the simplest everyday things, and now she whispered: "Please God, make him think I am still pretty."

The door opened and Jim stepped in and closed it. He looked thin and very serious. Poor fellow, he was only twenty-two–and to be burdened with a family! He needed a new overcoat and he was without gloves.

Jim stopped inside the door, as immovable as a setter at the scent of quail. His eyes were fixed upon Della, and there was an expression in them that she could not read, and it terrified her. It was not anger, nor surprise, nor disapproval, nor horror, nor any of the sentiments that she had been prepared for. He simply stared at her fixedly with that peculiar expression on his face.

Della wriggled off the table and went for him.

"Jim, darling," she cried, "don't look at me that way. I had my hair cut off and sold because I couldn't have lived through Christmas without giving you a present. It'll grow out again–you won't mind, will you? I just had to do it. My hair grows awfully fast. Say `Merry Christmas!' Jim, and let's be happy. You don't know what a nice–what a beautiful, nice gift I've got for you."

"You've cut off your hair?" asked Jim, laboriously, as if he had not arrived at that patent fact yet even after the hardest mental labor.

"Cut it off and sold it," said Della. "Don't you like me just as well, anyhow? I'm me without my hair, ain't I?"

Jim looked about the room curiously.

"You say your hair is gone?" he said, with an air almost of idiocy.

"You needn't look for it," said Della. "It's sold, I tell you–sold and gone, too. It's Christmas Eve, boy. Be good to me, for it went for you. Maybe the hairs of my head were numbered," she went on with sudden serious sweetness, "but nobody could ever count my love for you. Shall I put the chops on, Jim?"

Out of his trance Jim seemed quickly to wake. He enfolded his Della. For ten seconds let us regard with discreet scrutiny some inconsequential object in the other direction. Eight dollars a week or a million a year–what is the difference? A mathematician or a wit would give you the wrong answer. The magi brought valuable gifts, but that was not among them. This dark assertion will be illuminated later on.

Jim drew a package from his overcoat pocket and threw it upon the table.

"Don't make any mistake, Dell," he said, "about me. I don't think there's anything in the way of a haircut or a shave or a shampoo that could make me like my girl any less. But if you'll unwrap that package you may see why you had me going a while at first."

White fingers and nimble tore at the string and paper. And then an ecstatic scream of joy; and then, alas! a quick feminine change to hysterical tears and wails, necessitating the immediate employment of all the comforting powers of the lord of the flat.

For there lay The Combs–the set of combs, side and back, that Della had worshipped long in a Broadway window. Beautiful combs, pure tortoise shell, with jeweled rims–just the shade to wear in the beautiful vanished hair. They were expensive combs, she knew, and her heart had simply craved and yearned over them without the least hope of possession. And now, they were hers, but the tresses that should have adorned the coveted adornments were gone.

But she hugged them to her bosom, and at length she was able to look up with dim eyes and a smile and say: "My hair grows so fast, Jim!"

And then Della leaped up like a little singed cat and cried, "Oh, oh!"

Jim had not yet seen his beautiful present. She held it out to him eagerly upon her open palm. The dull precious metal seemed to flash with a reflection of her bright and ardent spirit.

"Isn't it a dandy, Jim? I hunted all over town to find it. You'll have to look at the time a hundred times a day now. Give me your watch. I want to see how it looks on it."

Instead of obeying, Jim tumbled down on the couch and put his hands under the back of his head and smiled.

"Dell," said he, "let's put our Christmas presents away and keep 'em a while. They're too nice to use just at present. I sold the watch to get the money to buy your combs. And now suppose you put the chops on."

The magi, as you know, were wise men—wonderfully wise men—who brought gifts to the Babe in the manger. They invented the art of giving Christmas presents. Being wise, their gifts were no doubt wise ones, possibly bearing the privilege of exchange in case of duplication. And here I have lamely related to you the uneventful chronicle of two foolish children in a flat who most unwisely sacrificed for each other the greatest treasures of their house. But in a last word to the wise of these days let it be said that of all who give gifts these two were the wisest. Of all who give and receive gifts, such as they are wisest. Everywhere they are wisest. They are the magi.

The Ransom *of* Red Chief

t looked like a good thing: but wait till I tell you. We were down South, in Alabama–Bill Driscoll and myself–when this kidnapping idea struck us. It was, as Bill afterward expressed it, "during a moment of temporary mental apparition"; but we didn't find that out till later.

There was a town down there, as flat as a flannel-cake, and called Summit, of course. It contained inhabitants of as undeleterious an self-satisfied a class of peasantry as ever clustered around a Maypole.

Bill and me had a joint capital of about six hundred dollars, and we needed just two thousand dollars more to pull off a fraudulent town-lot scheme in Western Illinois with. We talked it over on the front steps of the hotel. Philoprogenitiveness, says we, is strong in semi-rural communities; therefore, and for other reasons, a kidnapping project ought to do better there than in the radius of newspapers that send reporters out in plain clothes to stir up talk about such things. We knew that Summit couldn't get after us with anything stronger than constables and, maybe, some lackadaisical bloodhounds and a diatribe or two in the Weekly Farmers' Budget. So, it looked good.

We selected for our victim the only child of a prominent citizen named Ebenezer Dorset. The father was respectable and tight, a mortgage fancier and a stern, upright collection-plate passer and forecloser. The kid was a boy of ten, with bas-relief freckles, and hair the color of the cover of the magazine you buy at the newsstand when you want to catch a train. Bill and me figured that Ebenezer would melt down for a ransom of two thousand dollars to a cent. But wait till I tell you.

About two miles from Summit was a little mountain, covered with a dense cedar brake. On the rear elevation of this mountain was a cave. There we stored provisions.

One evening after sundown, we drove in a buggy past old Dorset's house.

The kid was in the street, throwing rocks at a kitten on the opposite fence.

"Hey, little boy!" says Bill, "would you like to have a bag of candy and a nice ride?"

The boy catches Bill neatly in the eye with a piece of brick.

"That will cost the old man an extra five hundred dollars," says Bill, climbing over the wheel.

That boy put up a fight like a welterweight cinnamon bear; but, at last, we got him down in the bottom of the buggy and drove away. We took him up to the cave, and I hitched the horse in the cedar brake. After dark I drove the buggy to the little village, three miles away, where we had hired it, and walked back to the mountain.

Bill was pasting court-plaster over the scratches and bruises on his features. There was a fire burning behind the big rock at the entrance of the cave, and the boy was watching a pot of boiling coffee, with two buzzard tail-feathers stuck in his red hair. He points a stick at me when I come up, and says:

"Ha! cursed paleface, do you dare to enter the camp of Red Chief, the terror of the plains?"

"He's all right now," says Bill, rolling up his trousers and examining some bruises on his shins. "We're playing Indian. We're making Buffalo Bill's show look like magic-lantern views of Palestine in the town hall. I'm Old Hank, the Trapper, Red Chief's captive, and I'm to be scalped at daybreak. By Geronimo! that kid can kick hard."

Yes, sir, that boy seemed to be having the time of his life. The fun of camping out in a cave had made him forget that he was a captive himself. He immediately christened me Snake-eye, the Spy, and announced that, when his braves returned from the warpath, I was to be broiled at the stake at the rising of the sun.

Then we had supper; and he filled his mouth full of bacon and bread and gravy, and began to talk. He made a during-dinner speech something like this:

"I like this fine. I never camped out before; but I had a pet 'possum once, and I was nine last birthday. I hate to go to school. Rats ate up sixteen of Jimmy Talbot's aunt's speckled hen's eggs. Are there any real Indians in these woods? I want some more gravy. Does the trees moving make the wind blow? We had five puppies. What makes your nose so red, Hank? My father has lots of money. Are the stars hot? I whipped Ed Walker twice, Saturday. I don't like girls. You dassent catch toads unless with a string. Do oxen make any noise? Why are oranges round? Have you got beds to sleep on in this cave? Amos Murray has got six toes. A parrot can talk, but a monkey or a fish can't. How many does it take to make twelve?"

Every few minutes he would remember that he was a pesky redskin, and pick up his stick rifle and tiptoe to the mouth of the cave to rubber for the scouts of the hated paleface. Now and then he would let out a war-whoop that made Old Hank the Trapper, shiver. That boy had Bill terrorized from the start.

"Red Chief," says I to the kid, "would you like to go home?"

"Aw, what for?" says he. "I don't have any fun at home. I hate to go to school. I like to camp out. You won't take me back home again, Snake-eye, will you?"

"Not right away," says I. "We'll stay here in the cave a while."

"All right!" says he. "That'll be fine. I never had such fun in all my life."

We went to bed about eleven o'clock. We spread down some wide blankets and quilts and put Red Chief between us. We weren't afraid he'd run away. He kept us awake for three hours, jumping up and reaching for his rifle and screeching: "Hist! pard," in mine and Bill's ears, as the fancied crackle of a twig or the rustle of a leaf revealed to his young imagination the stealthy approach of the outlaw band. At last, I fell into a troubled sleep, and dreamed that I had been kidnapped and chained to a tree by a ferocious pirate with red hair.

Just at daybreak, I was awakened by a series of awful screams from Bill. They weren't yells, or howls, or shouts, or whoops, or yawps, such as you'd expect from a manly set of vocal organs–they were simply indecent, terrifying, humiliating screams, such as women emit when they see ghosts or caterpillars. It's an awful thing to hear a strong, desperate, fat man scream incontinently in a cave at daybreak.

I jumped up to see what the matter was. Red Chief was sitting on Bill's chest, with one hand twined in Bill's hair. In the other he had the sharp case-knife we used for slicing bacon; and he was industriously and realistically trying to take Bill's scalp, according to the sentence that had been pronounced upon him the evening before.

I got the knife away from the kid and made him lie down again. But, from that moment, Bill's spirit was broken. He laid down on his side of the bed, but he never closed an eye again in sleep as long as that boy was with us. I dozed off for a while, but along toward sun-up I remembered that Red Chief had said I was to be burned at the stake at the rising of the sun. I wasn't nervous or afraid; but I sat up and lit my pipe and leaned against a rock.

"What you getting up so soon for, Sam?" asked Bill.

"Me?" says I. "Oh, I got a kind of a pain in my shoulder. I thought sitting up would rest it."

"You're a liar!" says Bill. "You're afraid. You was to be burned at sunrise, and you was afraid he'd do it. And he would, too, if he could find a match. Ain't it awful, Sam? Do you think anybody will pay out money to get a little imp like that back home?"

"Sure," said I. "A rowdy kid like that is just the kind that parents dote on. Now, you and the Chief get up and cook breakfast, while I go up on the top of this mountain and reconnoiter."

I went up on the peak of the little mountain and ran my eye over the contiguous vicinity. Over toward Summit I expected to see the sturdy yeomanry of the village armed with scythes and pitchforks beating the country-side for the dastardly kidnappers. But what I saw was a peaceful landscape dotted with one man ploughing with a dun mule. Nobody was dragging the creek; no couriers dashed hither and yon, bringing tidings of no news to the distracted parents. There was a sylvan attitude of somnolent sleepiness pervading that section of the external outward surface of Alabama that lay exposed to my view. "Perhaps," says I to myself, "it has not yet been discovered that the wolves have borne away the tender lambkin from the fold. Heaven help the wolves!" says I, and I went down the mountain to breakfast.

When I got to the cave I found Bill backed up against the side of it, breathing hard, and the boy threatening to smash him with a rock half as big as a cocoanut.

"He put a red-hot boiled potato down my back," explained Bill, "and then mashed it with his foot; and I boxed his ears. Have you got a gun about you, Sam?"

I took the rock away from the boy and kind of patched up the argument. "I'll fix you," says the kid to Bill. "No man ever yet struck the Red Chief but what he got paid for it. You better beware!"

After breakfast the kid takes a piece of leather with strings wrapped around it out of his pocket and goes outside the cave unwinding it.

"What's he up to now?" says Bill, anxiously. "You don't think he'll run away, do you, Sam?"

"No fear of it," says I. "He don't seem to be much of a home body. But we've got to fix up some plan about the ransom. There don't seem to be much excitement around Summit on account of his disappearance; but maybe they haven't realized yet that he's gone. His folks may think he's spending the night with Aunt Jane or one of the neighbors. Anyhow, he'll be missed today. Tonight we must get a message to his father demanding the two thousand dollars for his return."

Just then we heard a kind of war-whoop, such as David might have emitted when he knocked out the champion Goliath. It was a sling that Red Chief had pulled out of his pocket, and he was whirling it around his head.

I dodged, and heard a heavy thud and a kind of a sigh from Bill, like a horse gives out when you take his saddle off. A niggerhead rock the size of an egg had caught Bill just behind his left ear. He loosened himself all over and fell in the fire across the frying pan of hot water for washing the dishes. I dragged him out and poured cold water on his head for half an hour.

By and by, Bill sits up and feels behind his ear and says: "Sam, do you know who my favorite Biblical character is?"

"Take it easy," says I. "You'll come to your senses presently."

"King Herod," says he. "You won't go away and leave me here alone, will you, Sam?"

I went out and caught that boy and shook him until his freckles rattled.

"If you don't behave," says I, "I'll take you straight home. Now, are you going to be good, or not?"

"I was only funning," says he sullenly. "I didn't mean to hurt Old Hank. But what did he hit me for? I'll behave, Snake-eye, if you won't send me home, and if you'll let me play the Black Scout today."

"I don't know the game," says I. "That's for you and Mr. Bill to decide. He's your playmate for the day. I'm going away for a while, on business. Now, you come in and make friends with him and say you are sorry for hurting him, or home you go, at once."

I made him and Bill shake hands, and then I took Bill aside and told him I was going to Poplar Cove, a little village three miles from the cave, and find out what I could about how the kidnapping had been regarded in Summit. Also, I thought it best to send a peremptory letter to old man Dorset that day, demanding the ransom and dictating how it should be paid.

"You know, Sam," says Bill, "I've stood by you without batting an eye in earthquakes, fire, and flood—in poker games, dynamite outrages, police raids, train robberies, and cyclones. I never lost my nerve yet till we kidnapped that two-legged skyrocket of a kid. He's got me going. You won't leave me long with him, will you, Sam?"

"I'll be back some time this afternoon," says I. "You must keep the boy amused and quiet till I return. And now we'll write the letter to old Dorset."

Bill and I got paper and pencil and worked on the letter while Red Chief, with a blanket wrapped around him, strutted up and down, guarding the mouth of the cave. Bill begged me tearfully to make the ransom fifteen hundred dollars instead of two thousand. "I ain't attempting," says he, "to decry the celebrated moral aspect of parental affection, but we're dealing with humans, and it ain't human for anybody to give up two thousand dollars for that forty-pound chunk of freckled wildcat. I'm willing to take a chance at fifteen hundred dollars. You can charge the difference up to me."

So, to relieve Bill, I acceded, and we collaborated a letter that ran this way:

"Ebenezer Dorset, Esq.:

"We have your boy concealed in a place far from Summit. It is useless for you or the most skillful detectives to attempt to find him. Absolutely, the only terms on which you can have him restored to you are these: We demand fifteen hundred dollars in large bills for his return; the money to be left at midnight tonight at the same spot and in the same box as your reply—as hereinafter described. If you agree to these terms, send your answer in writing by a solitary messenger tonight at half-past eight o'clock. After crossing Owl Creek, on the road to Poplar Cove, there are three large trees about a hundred yards apart, close to the fence of the wheat field on the right-hand side. At the bottom of the fence-post, opposite the third tree, will be found a small pasteboard box.

"The messenger will place the answer in this box and return immediately to Summit.

"If you attempt any treachery or fail to comply with our demand as stated, you will never see your boy again.

"If you pay the money as demanded, he will be returned to you safe and well within three hours. These terms are final, and if you do not accede to them no further communication will be attempted.

Two Desperate Men"

I addressed this letter to Dorset, and put it in my pocket. As I was about to start, the kid comes up to me and says,

"Aw, Snake-eye, you said I could play the Black Scout while you was gone."

"Play it, of course," says I. "Mr. Bill will play with you. What kind of a game is it?"

"I'm the Black Scout," says Red Chief, "and I have to ride to the stockade to warn the settlers that the Indians are coming. I'm tired of playing Indian myself. I want to be the Black Scout."

"All right," says I. "It sounds harmless to me. I guess Mr. Bill will help you foil the pesky savages."

"What am I to do?" asks Bill, looking at the kid suspiciously.

"You are the hoss," says Black Scout. "Get down on your hands and knees. How can I ride to the stockade without a hoss?"

"You'd better keep him interested," said I, "till we get the scheme going. Loosen up."

Bill gets down on his all fours, and a look comes in his eye like a rabbit's when you catch it in a trap.

"How far is it to the stockade, kid?" he asks, in a husky manner of voice. "Ninety miles," says the Black Scout. "And you have to hump yourself to get there on time. Whoa, now!"

The Black Scout jumps on Bill's back and digs his heels in his side.

"For Heaven's sake," says Bill, "hurry back, Sam, as soon as you can. I wish we hadn't made the ransom more than a thousand. Say, you quit kicking me or I'll get up and warm you good."

I walked over to Poplar Cove and sat around the post-office and store, talking with the chawbacons that came in to trade. One whiskerando says that he hears Summit is all upset on account of Elder Ebenezer Dorset's boy having been lost or stolen. That was all I wanted to know. I bought some smoking tobacco, referred casually to the price of black-eyed peas, posted my letter surreptitiously, and came away. The postmaster said the mail-carrier would come by in an hour to take the mail on to Summit.

When I got back to the cave Bill and the boy were not to be found. I explored the vicinity of the cave, and risked a yodel or two, but there was no response.

So I lighted my pipe and sat down on a mossy bank to await developments.

In about half an hour I heard the bushes rustle, and Bill wabbled out into the little glade in front of the cave. Behind him was the kid, stepping softly like a scout, with a broad grin on his face. Bill stopped, took off his hat, and wiped his face with a red handkerchief. The kid stopped about eight feet behind him.

"Sam," says Bill, "I suppose you'll think I'm a renegade, but I couldn't help it. I'm a grown person with masculine proclivities and habits of self-defense, but there is a time when all systems of egotism and predominance fail. The boy is gone. I have sent him home. All is off. There was martyrs in old times," goes on Bill, "that suffered death rather than give up the particular graft they enjoyed. None of 'em ever was subjugated to such supernatural tortures as I have been. I tried to be faithful to our articles of depredation; but there came a limit."

"What's the trouble, Bill?" I asks him.

"I was rode," says Bill, "the ninety miles to the stockade, not barring an inch. Then, when the settlers was rescued, I was given oats. Sand ain't a palatable substitute. And then, for an hour I had to try to explain to him why there was nothin' in holes, how a road can run both ways, and what makes the grass green. I tell you, Sam, a human can only stand so much. I takes him by the neck of his clothes and drags him down the mountain. On the way he kicks my legs black-and-blue from the knees down; and I've got to have two or three bites on my thumb and hand cauterized.

"But he's gone"—continues Bill—"gone home. I showed him the road to Summit and kicked him about eight feet nearer there at one kick. I'm sorry we lose the ransom; but it was either that or Bill Driscoll to the madhouse."

Bill is puffing and blowing, but there is a look of ineffable peace and growing content on his rose-pink features.

"Bill," says I, "there isn't any heart disease in your family, is there?"

"No," says Bill, "nothing chronic except malaria and accidents. Why?"

"Then you might turn around," says I, "and have a look behind you."

Bill turns and sees the boy, and loses his complexion and sits down plump on the ground and begins to pluck aimlessly at grass and little sticks. For an hour I was afraid for his mind. And then I told him that my scheme was to put the whole job through immediately and that we would get the ransom and be off with it by midnight if old Dorset fell in with our proposition. So Bill braced up enough to give the kid a weak sort of a smile and a promise to play the Russian in a Japanese war with him as soon as he felt a little better.

I had a scheme for collecting that ransom without danger of being caught by counterplots that ought to commend itself to professional kidnappers. The tree under which the answer was to be left—and the money later on—was close to the road fence with big, bare fields on all sides. If a gang of constables should be watching for anyone to come for the note, they could see him a long way off crossing the fields or in the road. But no, sirree! At half-past eight I was up in that tree as well hidden as a tree toad, waiting for the messenger to arrive.

Exactly on time, a half-grown boy rides up the road on a bicycle, locates the pasteboard box at the foot of the fence-post, slips a folded piece of paper into it, and pedals away again back toward Summit.

I waited an hour and then concluded the thing was square. I slid down the tree, got the note, slipped along the fence till I struck the woods, and was back at the cave in another half an hour. I opened the note, got near the lantern, and read it to Bill. It was written with a pen in a crabbed hand, and the sum and substance of it was this:

"Gentlemen: I received your letter today by post, in regard to the ransom you ask for the return of my son. I think you are a little high in your demands, and I hereby make you a counter-proposition, which I am inclined to believe you will accept. You bring Johnny home and pay me two hundred and fifty dollars in cash, and I agree to take him off your hands. You had better come at night, for the neighbors believe he is lost, and I couldn't be responsible for what they would do to anybody they saw bringing him back.

Very respectfully, Ebenezer Dorset

"Great pirates of Penzance!" says I; "of all the impudent—"

But I glanced at Bill, and hesitated. He had the most appealing look in his eyes I ever saw on the face of a dumb or a talking brute.

"Sam," says he, "what's two hundred and fifty dollars, after all? We've got the money. One more night of this kid will send me to a bed in Bedlam. Besides being a thorough gentleman, I think Mr. Dorset is a spendthrift for making us such a liberal offer. You ain't going to let the chance go, are you?"

"Tell you the truth, Bill," says I, "this little he-ewe lamb has somewhat got on my nerves too. We'll take him home, pay the ransom, and make our getaway."

We took him home that night. We got him to go by telling him that his father had bought a silver-mounted rifle and a pair of moccasins for him, and we were going to hunt bears the next day.

It was just twelve o 'clock when we knocked at Ebenezer's front door. Just at the moment when I should have been abstracting the fifteen hundred dollars from the box under the tree, according to the original proposition, Bill was counting out two hundred and fifty dollars into Dorset's hand.

When the kid found out we were going to leave him at home he started up a howl like a calliope and fastened himself as tight as a leech to Bill's leg. His father peeled him away gradually, like a porous plaster.

"How long can you hold him?" asks Bill.

"I'm not as strong as I used to be," says old Dorset, "but I think I can promise you ten minutes."

"Enough," says Bill. "In ten minutes I shall cross the Central, Southern, and Middle Western States, and be legging it trippingly for the Canadian border."

And, as dark as it was, and as fat as Bill was, and as good a runner as I am, he was a good mile and a half out of Summit before I could catch up with him.

The Last *of* The Troubadours

nexorably Sam Galloway saddled his pony. He was going away from the Rancho Altito at the end of a three-months' visit. It is not to be expected that a guest should put up with wheat coffee and biscuits yellow-streaked with saleratus[1] for longer than that. Nick Napoleon, the big Negro man cook, had never been able to make good biscuits. Once before, when Nick was cooking at the Willow Ranch, Sam had been forced to fly from his cuisine, after only a six-weeks' sojourn.

On Sam's face was an expression of sorrow, deepened with regret and slightly tempered by the patient forgiveness of a connoisseur who cannot be understood. But very firmly and inexorably he buckled his saddle-cinches, looped his stake-rope and hung it to his saddle-horn, tied his slicker and coat on the cantle, and looped his quirt on his right wrist. The Merrydews (householders of the Rancho Altito), men, women, children, and servants, vassals, visitors, employees, dogs, and casual callers were grouped in the "gallery" of the ranch house, all with faces set to the tune of melancholy and grief. For, as the coming of Sam Galloway to any ranch, camp, or cabin between the rivers Frio or Bravo del Norte aroused joy, so his departure caused mourning and distress.

And then, during absolute silence, except for the bumping of a hind elbow of a hound dog as he pursued a wicked flea, Sam tenderly and carefully tied his guitar across his saddle on top of his slicker and coat. The guitar was in a green duck bag; and if you catch the significance of it, it explains Sam.

Sam Galloway was the Last of the Troubadours. Of course you know about the troubadours. The encyclopedia says they flourished between the eleventh and the thirteenth centuries. What they flourished doesn't seem clear—you may be pretty sure it wasn't a sword: maybe it was a fiddlebow, or a forkful of spaghetti, or a lady's scarf. Anyhow, Sam Galloway was one of 'em.

Sam put on a martyred expression as he mounted his pony. But the expression on his face was hilarious compared with the one on his pony's. You see, a pony gets to know his rider mighty well, and it is not unlikely that cow ponies in pastures and at hitching racks had often guyed Sam's pony for being ridden by a guitar player instead of by a rollicking, cussing, all-wool cowboy. No man is a hero to his saddle-horse. And even an escalator in a department store might be excused for tripping up a troubadour.

Oh, I know I'm one; and so are you. You remember the stories you memorize and the card tricks you study and that little piece on the piano—how does it go?—ti-tum-te-tum-ti-tum—those little Arabian Ten Minute Entertainments that you furnish when you go up to call on your rich Aunt Jane. You should know that *omnae personae in tres partes divisae sunt*. Namely: Barons, Troubadours, and Workers. Barons have no inclination to read such folderol as this; and Workers have no time: so I know you

---

[1] *another name for sodium bicarbonate -*

must be a Troubadour, and that you will understand Sam Galloway. Whether we sing, act, dance, write, lecture, or paint, we are only troubadours; so let us make the worst of it.

The pony with the Dante Alighieri face, guided by the pressure of Sam's knees, bore that wandering minstrel sixteen miles southeastward. Nature was in her most benignant mood. League after league of delicate, sweet flowerets made fragrant the gently undulating prairie. The east wind tempered the spring warmth; wool-white clouds flying in from the Mexican Gulf hindered the direct rays of the April sun. Sam sang songs as he rode. Under his pony's bridle he had tucked some sprigs of chaparral to keep away the deer flies. Thus crowned, the long-faced quadruped looked more Dantesque than before, and, judging by his countenance, seemed to think of Beatrice.

Straight as topography permitted, Sam rode to the sheep ranch of old man Ellison. A visit to a sheep ranch seemed to him desirable just then. There had been too many people, too much noise, argument, competition, confusion, at Rancho Altito. He had never conferred upon old man Ellison the favor of sojourning at his ranch; but he knew he would be welcome. The troubadour is his own passport everywhere. The Workers in the castle let down the drawbridge to him, and the Baron sets him at his left hand at table in the banquet hall. There ladies smile upon him and applaud his songs and stories, while the Workers bring boars' heads and flagons. If the Baron nods once or twice in his carved oaken chair, he does not do it maliciously.

Old man Ellison welcomed the troubadour flatteringly. He had often heard praises of Sam Galloway from other ranchmen who had been complimented by his visits, but had never aspired to such an honor for his own humble barony. I say barony because old man Ellison was the Last of the Barons. Of course, Mr. Bulwer-Lytton lived too early to know him, or he wouldn't have conferred that sobriquet upon Warwick. In life it is the duty and the function of the Baron to provide work for the Workers and lodging and shelter for the Troubadours.

Old man Ellison was a shrunken old man, with a short, yellow-white beard and a face lined and seamed by past-and-gone smiles. His ranch was a little two-room box house in a grove of hackberry trees in the lonesomest part of the sheep country. His household consisted of a Kiowa Indian man cook, four hounds, a pet sheep, and a half-tamed coyote chained to a fence-post. He owned 3,000 sheep, which he ran on two sections of leased land and many thousands of acres neither leased nor owned. Three or four times a year someone who spoke his language would ride up to his gate and exchange a few bald ideas with him. Those were red-letter days to old man Ellison. Then in what illuminated, embossed, and gorgeously decorated capitals must have been written the day on which a troubadour–a troubadour who, according to the encyclopedia, should have flourished between the eleventh and the thirteenth centuries–drew rein at the gates of his baronial castle!

Old man Ellison's smiles came back and filled his wrinkles when he saw Sam. He hurried out of the house in his shuffling, limping way to greet him.

"Hello, Mr. Ellison," called Sam cheerfully. "Thought I'd drop over and see you a while. Notice you've had fine rains on your range. They ought to make good grazing for your spring lambs."

"Well, well, well," said old man Ellison. "I'm mighty glad to see you, Sam. I never thought you'd take the trouble to ride over to as out-of-the-way an old ranch as this. But you're mighty welcome. 'Light. I've got a sack of new oats in the kitchen—shall I bring out a feed for your hoss?"

"Oats for him?" said Sam, derisively. "No, sir-ee. He's as fat as a pig now on grass. He don't get rode enough to keep him in condition. I'll just turn him in the horse pasture with a drag rope on if you don't mind."

I am positive that never during the eleventh and thirteenth centuries did Baron, Troubadour, and Worker amalgamate as harmoniously as their parallels did that evening at old man Ellison's sheep ranch. The Kiowa's biscuits were light and tasty and his coffee strong. Ineradicable hospitality and appreciation glowed on old man Ellison's weather-tanned face. As for the troubadour, he said to himself that he had stumbled upon pleasant places indeed. A well-cooked, abundant meal, a host whom his lightest attempt to entertain seemed to delight far beyond the merits of the exertion, and the reposeful atmosphere that his sensitive soul at that time craved united to confer upon him a satisfaction and luxurious ease that he had seldom found on his tours of the ranches.

After the delectable supper, Sam untied the green duck bag and took out his guitar. Not by way of payment, mind you—neither Sam Galloway nor any other of the true troubadours are lineal descendants of the late Tommy Tucker. You have read of Tommy Tucker in the works of the esteemed but often obscure Mother Goose. Tommy Tucker sang for his supper. No true troubadour would do that. He would have his supper, and then sing for Art's sake.

Sam Galloway's repertoire comprised about fifty funny stories and between thirty and forty songs. He by no means stopped there. He could talk through twenty cigarettes on any topic that you brought up. And he never sat up when he could lie down; and never stood when he could sit. I am strongly disposed to linger with him, for I am drawing a portrait as well as a blunt pencil and a tattered thesaurus will allow.

I wish you could have seen him: he was small and tough and inactive beyond the power of imagination to conceive. He wore an ultramarine-blue woolen shirt laced down the front with a pearl-gray, exaggerated sort of shoestring, indestructible brown duck clothes, inevitable high-heeled boots with Mexican spurs, and a Mexican straw sombrero.

That evening Sam and old man Ellison dragged their chairs out under the hackberry trees. They lighted cigarettes; and the troubadour gaily touched his guitar. Many of the songs he sang were the weird, melancholy, minor-keyed *canciones* that he had learned from the Mexican sheepherders and vaqueros. One, in particular, charmed and soothed the soul of the lonely baron. It was a favorite song of the sheepherders, beginning: "*Huile, huile, palomita,*" which being translated means, "Fly, fly, little dove." Sam sang it for old man Ellison many times that evening.

The troubadour stayed on at the old man's ranch. There was peace and quiet and appreciation there, such as he had not found in the noisy camps of the cattle kings. No audience in the world could have crowned the work of poet, musician, or artist with more worshipful and unflagging approval than that bestowed upon his efforts by old man Ellison. No visit by a royal personage to a humble woodchopper or peasant could have been received with more flattering thankfulness and joy.

On a cool, canvas-covered cot in the shade of the hackberry trees Sam Galloway passed the greater part of his time. There he rolled his brown paper cigarettes, read such tedious literature as the ranch afforded, and added to his repertoire of improvisations that he played so expertly on his guitar. To him, as a slave ministering to a great lord, the Kiowa brought cool water from the red jar hanging under the brush shelter, and food when he called for it. The prairie zephyrs fanned him mildly; mocking-birds at morn and eve competed with but scarce equaled the sweet melodies of his lyre; a perfumed stillness seemed to fill all his world. While old man Ellison was pottering among his flocks of sheep on his mile-an-hour pony, and while the Kiowa took his siesta in the burning sunshine at the end of the kitchen, Sam would lie on his cot thinking what a happy world he lived in, and how kind it is to the ones whose mission in life it is to give entertainment and pleasure. Here he had food and lodging as good as he had ever longed for; absolute immunity from care or exertion or strife; an endless welcome, and a host whose delight at the sixteenth repetition of a song or a story was as keen as at its initial giving. Was there ever a troubadour of old who struck upon as royal a castle in his wanderings? While he lay thus, meditating upon his blessings, little brown cottontails would shyly frolic through the yard; a covey of white-topknotted blue quail would run past, in single file, twenty yards away; a *paisano* bird, out hunting for tarantulas, would hop upon the fence and salute him with sweeping flourishes of its long tail. In the eighty-acre horse pasture the pony with the Dantesque face grew fat and almost smiling. The troubadour was at the end of his wanderings.

Old man Ellison was his own *vaciero*. That means that he supplied his sheep camps with wood, water, and rations by his own labors instead of hiring a *vaciero*. On small ranches it is often done.

One morning he started for the camp of Incarnacion Felipe de la Cruz y Monte Piedras (one of his sheep herders) with the week's usual rations of brown beans, coffee, meal, and sugar. Two miles away on the trail from old Fort Ewing he met, face to face, a terrible being called King James, mounted on a fiery, prancing, Kentucky-bred horse.

King James's real name was James King; but people reversed it because it seemed to fit him better, and also because it seemed to please his majesty. King James was the biggest cattleman between the Alamo plaza in San Antone and Bill Hopper's saloon in Brownsville. Also he was the loudest and most offensive bully and braggart and bad man in southwest Texas. And he always made good whenever he bragged; and the more noise he made the more dangerous he was. In the story papers it is always the quiet, mild-mannered man with light blue eyes and a low voice who turns out to be really dangerous; but in real life and in this story such is not the case. Give me my choice between assaulting a large, loudmouthed roughhouser and an inoffensive stranger with blue eyes sitting quietly in a corner, and you will see something doing in the corner every time.

King James, as I intended to say earlier, was a fierce, two-hundred-pound, sunburned, blond man, as pink as an October strawberry, and with two horizontal slits under shaggy red eyebrows for eyes. On that day he wore a flannel shirt that was tan-colored, with the exception of certain large areas which were darkened by transudations due to the summer sun. There seemed to be other clothing and garnishings about him, such as brown duck trousers stuffed into immense boots, and red handkerchiefs and revolvers; and a shotgun laid across his saddle and a leather belt with millions of cartridges shining in it–but your mind skidded off such accessories; what held your gaze was just the two little horizontal slits that he used for eyes.

This was the man that old man Ellison met on the trail; and when you count up in the baron's favor that he was sixty-five and weighed ninety-eight pounds and had heard of King James's record and that he (the baron) had a hankering for the vita simplex and had no gun with him and wouldn't have used it if he had, you can't censure him if I tell you that the smiles with which the troubadour had filled his wrinkles went out of them and left them plain wrinkles again. But he was not the kind of baron that flies from danger. He reined in the mile-an-hour pony (no difficult feat), and saluted the formidable monarch.

King James expressed himself with royal directness. "You're that old snoozer that's running sheep on this range, ain't you?" said he. "What right have you got to do it? Do you own any land, or lease any?"

"I have two sections leased from the state," said old man Ellison, mildly.

"Not by no means you haven't," said King James. "Your lease expired yesterday; and I had a man at the land office on the minute to take it up. You don't control a foot of grass in Texas. You sheep men have got to git. Your time's up. It's a cattle country, and there ain't any room in it for snoozers. This range you've got your sheep on is mine. I'm putting up a wire fence, forty by sixty miles; and if there's a sheep inside of it when it's done it'll be a dead one. I'll give you a week to move yours away. If they ain't gone by then, I'll send six men over here with Winchesters to make mutton out of the whole lot. And if I find you here at the same time this is what you'll get."

King James patted the breech of his shotgun warningly.

Old man Ellison rode on to the camp of Incarnacion. He sighed many times, and the wrinkles in his face grew deeper. Rumors that the old order was about to change had reached him before. The end of Free Grass was in sight. Other troubles, too, had been accumulating upon his shoulders. His flocks were decreasing instead of growing; the price of wool was declining at every clip; even Bradshaw, the storekeeper at Frio City, at whose store he bought his ranch supplies, was dunning him for his last six months' bill and threatening to cut him off. And so this last greatest calamity suddenly dealt out to him by the terrible King James was a crusher.

When the old man got back to the ranch at sunset he found Sam Galloway lying on his cot, propped against a roll of blankets and woolsacks, fingering his guitar.

"Hello, Uncle Ben," the troubadour called, cheerfully. "You rolled in early this evening. I been trying a new twist on the Spanish Fandango today. I just about got it. Here's how she goes—listen."

"That's fine, that's mighty fine," said old man Ellison, sitting on the kitchen step and rubbing his white, Scotch-terrier whiskers. "I reckon you've got all the musicians beat east and west, Sam, as far as the roads are cut out."

"Oh, I don't know," said Sam, reflectively. "But I certainly do get there on variations. I guess I can handle anything in five flats about as well as any of 'em. But you look kind of fagged out, Uncle Ben—ain't you feeling right well this evening?"

"Little tired; that's all, Sam. If you ain't played yourself out, let's have that Mexican piece that starts off with: '*Huile, huile, palomita*.' It seems that that song always kind of soothes and comforts me after I've been riding far or anything bothers me."

"Why, *seguramente*, senor," said Sam. "I'll hit her up for you as often as you like. And before I forget about it, Uncle Ben, you want to jerk Bradshaw up about them last hams he sent us. They're just a little bit strong."

A man sixty-five years old, living on a sheep ranch and beset by a complication of disasters, cannot successfully and continuously dissemble. Moreover, a troubadour has eyes quick to see unhappiness in others around him–because it disturbs his own ease. So, on the next day, Sam again questioned the old man about his air of sadness and abstraction. Then old man Ellison told him the story of King James's threats and orders and that pale melancholy and red ruin appeared to have marked him for their own. The troubadour took the news thoughtfully. He had heard much about King James.

On the third day of the seven days of grace allowed him by the autocrat of the range, old man Ellison drove his buckboard to Frio City to fetch some necessary supplies for the ranch. Bradshaw was hard but not implacable. He divided the old man's order by two, and let him have a little more time. One article secured was a new, fine ham for the pleasure of the troubadour.

Five miles out of Frio City on his way home the old man met King James riding into town. His majesty could never look anything but fierce and menacing, but today his slits of eyes appeared to be a little wider than they usually were.

"Good day," said the king, gruffly. "I've been wanting to see you. I hear it said by a cowman from Sandy yesterday that you was from Jackson County, Mississippi, originally. I want to know if that's a fact."

"Born there," said old man Ellison, "and raised there till I was twenty-one."

"This man says," went on King James, "that he thinks you was related to the Jackson County Reeveses. Was he right?"

"Aunt Caroline Reeves," said the old man, "was my half-sister."

"She was my aunt," said King James. "I run away from home when I was sixteen. Now, let's re-talk over some things that we discussed a few days ago. They call me a bad man; and they're only half right. There's plenty of room in my pasture for your bunch of sheep and their increase for a long time to come. Aunt Caroline used to cut out sheep in cake dough and bake 'em for me. You keep your sheep where they are, and use all the range you want. How's your finances?"

The old man related his woes in detail, dignifiedly, with restraint and candor.

"She used to smuggle extra grub into my school basket–I'm speaking of Aunt Caroline," said King James. "I'm going over to Frio City today, and I'll ride back by your ranch tomorrow. I'll draw $2,000 out of the bank there and bring it over to you; and I'll tell Bradshaw to let you have everything you want on credit. You are bound to have heard the old saying at home, that the Jackson County Reeveses and Kings would stick closer by each other than chestnut burrs. Well, I'm a King yet whenever I run across a Reeves. So you look out for me along about sundown tomorrow, and don't worry about nothing. Shouldn't wonder if the dry spell don't kill out the young grass."

Old man Ellison drove happily ranchward. Once more the smiles filled out his wrinkles. Very suddenly, by the magic of kinship and the good that lies somewhere in all hearts, his troubles had been removed.

On reaching the ranch he found that Sam Galloway was not there. His guitar hung by its buckskin string to a hackberry limb, moaning as the gulf breeze blew across its masterless strings.

The Kiowa endeavored to explain.

"Sam, he catch pony," said he, "and say he ride to Frio City. What for no can damn *sabe*. Say he come back tonight. Maybe so. That all."

As the first stars came out the troubadour rode back to his haven. He pastured his pony and went into the house, his spurs jingling martially.

Old man Ellison sat at the kitchen table, having a tin cup of before-supper coffee. He looked contented and pleased.

"Hello, Sam," said he. "I'm darned glad to see ye back. I don't know how I managed to get along on this ranch, anyhow, before ye dropped in to cheer things up. I'll bet ye've been skylarking around with some of them Frio City gals, now, that's kept ye so late."

And then old man Ellison took another look at Sam's face and saw that the minstrel had changed to the man of action.

And while Sam is unbuckling from his waist old man Ellison's six-shooter, that the latter had left behind when he drove to town, we may well pause to remark that anywhere and whenever a troubadour lays down the guitar and takes up the sword trouble is sure to follow. It is not the expert thrust of Athos nor the cold skill of Aramis nor the iron wrist of Porthos that we have to fear–it is the Gascon's fury–the wild and unacademic attack of the troubadour–the sword of D'Artagnan.

"I done it," said Sam. "I went over to Frio City to do it. I couldn't let him put the skibunk on you, Uncle Ben. I met him in Summers's saloon. I knowed what to do. I said a few things to him that nobody else heard. He reached for his gun first–half a dozen fellows saw him do it–but I got mine unlimbered first. Three doses I gave him–right around the lungs, and a saucer could have covered up all of 'em. He won't bother you no more."

"This–is–King–James–you speak–of?" asked old man Ellison, while he sipped his coffee.

"You bet it was. And they took me before the county judge; and the witnesses what saw him draw his gun first was all there. Well, of course, they put me under $300 bond to appear before the court, but there was four or five boys on the spot ready to sign the bail. He won't bother you no more, Uncle Ben. You ought to have seen how close them bullet holes was together. I reckon playing a guitar as much as I do must kind of limber a fellow's trigger finger up a little, don't you think, Uncle Ben?"

Then there was a little silence in the castle except for the spluttering of a venison steak that the Kiowa was cooking.

"Sam," said old man Ellison, stroking his white whiskers with a tremulous hand, "would you mind getting the guitar and playing that '*Huile, huile, palomita*' piece once or twice? It always seems to be kind of soothing and comforting when a man's tired and fagged out."

There is no more to be said, except that the title of the story is wrong. It should have been called "The Last of the Barons." There never will be an end to the troubadours; and now and then it does seem that the jingle of their guitars will drown the sound of the muffled blows of the pickaxes and trip hammers of all the Workers in the world.

The Sleuths

n The Big City a man will disappear with the suddenness and completeness of the flame of a candle that is blown out. All the agencies of inquisition–the hounds of the trail, the sleuths of the city's labyrinths, the closet detectives of theory and induction–will be invoked to the search. Most often the man's face will be seen no more. Sometimes he will reappear in Sheboygan or in the wilds of Terre Haute, calling himself one of the synonyms of "Smith," and without memory of events up to a certain time, including his grocer's bill. Sometimes it will be found, after dragging the rivers, and polling the restaurants to see if he may be waiting for a well-done sirloin, that he has moved next door.

This snuffing out of a human being like the erasure of a chalk man from a blackboard is one of the most impressive themes in dramaturgy.

The case of Mary Snyder, in point, should not be without interest.

A man of middle age, of the name of Meeks, came from the West to New York to find his sister, Mrs. Mary Snyder, a widow, aged fifty-two, who had been living for a year in a tenement house in a crowded neighborhood.

At her address he was told that Mary Snyder had moved away longer than a month before. No one could tell him her new address.

On coming out Mr. Meeks addressed a policeman who was standing on the corner, and explained his dilemma.

"My sister is very poor," he said, "and I am anxious to find her. I have recently made quite a lot of money in a lead mine, and I want her to share my prosperity. There is no use in advertising her, because she cannot read."

The policeman pulled his moustache and looked so thoughtful and mighty that Meeks could almost feel the joyful tears of his sister Mary dropping upon his bright blue tie.

"You go down in the Canal Street neighborhood," said the policeman, "and get a job drivin' the biggest dray you can find. There's old women always gettin' knocked over by drays down there. You might see 'er among 'em. If you don't want to do that you better go 'round to headquarters and get 'em to put a fly cop onto the dame."

At police headquarters, Meeks received ready assistance. A general alarm was sent out, and copies of a photograph of Mary Snyder that her brother had were distributed among the stations. In Mulberry Street the chief assigned Detective Mullins to the case.

The detective took Meeks aside and said:

"This is not a very difficult case to unravel. Shave off your whiskers, fill your pockets with good cigars, and meet me in the cafe of the Waldorf at three o'clock this afternoon."

Meeks obeyed. He found Mullins there. They had a bottle of wine, while the detective asked questions concerning the missing woman.

"Now," said Mullins, "New York is a big city, but we've got the detective business systematized. There are two ways we can go about finding your sister. We will try one of 'em first. You say she's fifty-two?"

"A little past," said Meeks.

The detective conducted the Westerner to a branch advertising office of one of the largest dailies. There he wrote the following "ad" and submitted it to Meeks:

"Wanted, at once—one hundred attractive chorus girls for a new musical comedy. Apply all day at No. — Broadway."

Meeks was indignant.

"My sister," said he, "is a poor, hard-working, elderly woman. I do not see what aid an advertisement of this kind would be toward finding her."

"All right," said the detective. "I guess you don't know New York. But if you've got a grouch against this scheme we'll try the other one. It's a sure thing. But it'll cost you more."

"Never mind the expense," said Meeks; "we'll try it."

The sleuth led him back to the Waldorf. "Engage a couple of bedrooms and a parlor," he advised, "and let's go up."

This was done, and the two were shown to a superb suite on the fourth floor. Meeks looked puzzled. The detective sank into a velvet armchair, and pulled out his cigar case.

"I forgot to suggest, old man," he said, "that you should have taken the rooms by the month. They wouldn't have stuck you so much for 'em.

"By the month!" exclaimed Meeks. "What do you mean?"

"Oh, it'll take time to work the game this way. I told you it would cost you more. We'll have to wait till spring. There'll be a new city directory out then. Very likely your sister's name and address will be in it."

Meeks rid himself of the city detective at once. On the next day someone advised him to consult Shamrock Jolnes, New York's famous private detective, who demanded fabulous fees, but performed miracles in the way of solving mysteries and crimes.

After waiting for two hours in the anteroom of the great detective's apartment, Meeks was shown into his presence. Jolnes sat in a purple dressing gown at an inlaid ivory chess table, with a magazine before him, trying to solve the mystery of "They." The famous sleuth's thin, intellectual face, piercing eyes, and rate per word are too well known to need description.

Meeks set forth his errand. "My fee, if successful, will be $500," said Shamrock Jolnes.

Meeks bowed his agreement to the price.

"I will undertake your case, Mr. Meeks," said Jolnes, finally. "The disappearance of people in this city has always been an interesting problem to me. I remember a case that I brought to a successful outcome a year ago. A family bearing the name of Clark disappeared suddenly from a small flat in which they were living. I watched the flat building for two months for a clue. One day it struck me that a certain milkman and a grocer's boy always walked backward when they carried their wares upstairs. Following out by induction the idea that this observation gave me, I at once located the missing family. They had moved into the flat across the hall and changed their name to Kralc."

Shamrock Jolnes and his client went to the tenement house where Mary Snyder had lived, and the detective demanded to be shown the room in which she had lived. It had been occupied by no tenant since her disappearance.

The room was small, dingy, and poorly furnished. Meeks seated himself dejectedly on a broken chair, while the great detective searched the walls and floor and the few sticks of old, rickety furniture for a clue.

At the end of half an hour Jolnes had collected a few seemingly unintelligible articles–a cheap black hatpin, a piece torn off a theatre program, and the end of a small torn card on which was the word "left" and the characters "C 12."

Shamrock Jolnes leaned against the mantel for ten minutes, with his head resting upon his hand, and an absorbed look upon his intellectual face. At the end of that time he exclaimed, with animation:

"Come, Mr. Meeks; the problem is solved. I can take you directly to the house where your sister is living. And you may have no fears concerning her welfare, for she is amply provided with funds–for the present at least."

Meeks felt joy and wonder in equal proportions.

"How did you manage it?" he asked, with admiration in his tones.

Perhaps Jolnes's only weakness was a professional pride in his wonderful achievements in induction. He was ever ready to astound and charm his listeners by describing his methods.

"By elimination," said Jolnes, spreading his clues upon a little table, "I got rid of certain parts of the city to which Mrs. Snyder might have removed. You see this hatpin? That eliminates Brooklyn. No woman attempts to board a car at the Brooklyn Bridge without being sure that she carries a hatpin with which to fight her way into a seat. And now I will demonstrate to you that she could not have gone to Harlem. Behind this door are two hooks in the wall. Upon one of these Mrs. Snyder has hung her bonnet, and upon the other her shawl. You will observe that the bottom of the hanging shawl has gradually made a soiled streak against the plastered wall. The mark is clean-cut, proving that there is no fringe on the shawl. Now, was there ever a case where a middle-aged woman, wearing a shawl, boarded a Harlem train without there being a fringe on the shawl to catch in the gate and delay the passengers behind her? So we eliminate Harlem.

"Therefore I conclude that Mrs. Snyder has not moved very far away. On this torn piece of card you see the word 'Left,' the letter 'C,' and the number '12.' Now, I happen to know that No. 12 Avenue C is a first-class boarding house, far beyond your sister's means–as we suppose. But then I find this piece of a theatre program, crumpled into an odd shape. What meaning does it convey? None to you, very likely, Mr. Meeks; but it is eloquent to one whose habits and training take cognizance of the smallest things.

"You have told me that your sister was a scrub woman. She scrubbed the floors of offices and hallways. Let us assume that she procured such work to perform in a theatre. Where is valuable jewelry lost the oftenest, Mr. Meeks? In the theatres, of course. Look at that piece of program, Mr. Meeks. Observe the round impression in it. It has been wrapped around a ring– perhaps a ring of great value. Mrs. Snyder found the ring while at work in the theatre. She hastily tore off a piece of a program, wrapped the ring carefully, and thrust it into her bosom. The next day she disposed of it, and, with her increased means, looked about her for a more comfortable place in which to live. When I reach thus far in the chain I see nothing impossible about No. 12 Avenue C. It is there we will find your sister, Mr. Meeks."

Shamrock Jolnes concluded his convincing speech with the smile of a successful artist. Meeks' admiration was too great for words. Together they went to No. 12 Avenue C. It was an old-fashioned brownstone house in a prosperous and respectable neighborhood.

They rang the bell, and on inquiring were told that no Mrs. Snyder was known there, and that not within six months had a new occupant come to the house.

When they reached the sidewalk again, Meeks examined the clues which he had brought away from his sister's old room.

"I am no detective," he remarked to Jolnes as he raised the piece of theatre program to his nose, "but it seems to me that instead of a ring having been wrapped in this paper it was one of those round peppermint drops. And this piece with the address on it looks to me like the end of a seat coupon–No. 12, row C, left aisle."

Shamrock Jolnes had a far-away look in his eyes.

"I think you would do well to consult Juggins," said he.

"Who is Juggins?" asked Meeks.

"He is the leader," said Jolnes, "of a new modern school of detectives. Their methods are different from ours, but it is said that Juggins has solved some extremely puzzling cases. I will take you to him."

They found the greater Juggins in his office. He was a small man with light hair, deeply absorbed in reading one of the bourgeois works of Nathaniel Hawthorne.

The two great detectives of different schools shook hands with ceremony, and Meeks was introduced.

"State the facts," said Juggins, going on with his reading.

When Meeks ceased, the greater one closed his book and said:

"Do I understand that your sister is fifty-two years of age, with a large mole on the side of her nose, and that she is a very poor widow, making a scanty living by scrubbing, and with a very homely face and figure?"

"That describes her exactly," admitted Meeks. Juggins rose and put on his hat.

"In fifteen minutes," he said, "I will return, bringing you her present address."

Shamrock Jolnes turned pale, but forced a smile.

Within the specified time Juggins returned and consulted a little slip of paper held in his hand.

"Your sister, Mary Snyder," he announced calmly, "will be found at No. 162 Chilton Street. She is living in the back hall bedroom, five flights up. The house is only four blocks from here," he continued, addressing Meeks. "Suppose you go and verify the statement and then return here. Mr. Jolnes will await you, I dare say."

Meeks hurried away. In twenty minutes he was back again, with a beaming face.

"She is there and well!" he cried. "Name your fee!"

"Two dollars," said Juggins.

When Meeks had settled his bill and departed, Shamrock Jolnes stood with his hat in his hand before Juggins.

"If it would not be asking too much," he stammered–"if you would favor me so far–would you object to–"

"Certainly not," said Juggins pleasantly. "I will tell you how I did it. You remember the description of Mrs. Snyder? Did you ever know a woman like that who wasn't paying weekly installments on an enlarged crayon portrait of herself? The biggest factory of that kind in the country is just around the corner. I went there and got her address off the books. That's all."

Witches' Loaves

iss Martha Meacham kept the little bakery on the corner (the one where you go up three steps, and the bell tinkles when you open the door).

Miss Martha was forty, her bankbook showed a credit of two thousand dollars, and she possessed two false teeth and a sympathetic heart. Many people have married whose chances to do so were much inferior to Miss Martha's.

Two or three times a week a customer came in in whom she began to take an interest. He was a middle-aged man, wearing spectacles and a brown beard trimmed to a careful point.

He spoke English with a strong German accent. His clothes were worn and darned in places, and wrinkled and baggy in others. But he looked neat, and had very good manners.

He always bought two loaves of stale bread. Fresh bread was five cents a loaf. Stale ones were two for five. Never did he call for anything but stale bread.

Once Miss Martha saw a red and brown stain on his fingers. She was sure then that he was an artist and very poor. No doubt he lived in a garret, where he painted pictures and ate stale bread and thought of the good things to eat in Miss Martha's bakery.

Often when Miss Martha sat down to her chops and light rolls and jam and tea she would sigh, and wish that the gentle-mannered artist might share her tasty meal instead of eating his dry crust in that draughty attic. Miss Martha's heart, as you have been told, was a sympathetic one.

In order to test her theory as to his occupation, she brought from her room one day a painting that she had bought at a sale, and set it against the shelves behind the bread counter.

It was a Venetian scene. A splendid marble *palazzio* (so it said on the picture) stood in the foreground—or rather forewater. For the rest there were gondolas (with the lady trailing her hand in the water), clouds, sky, and *chiaro-oscuro* in plenty. No artist could fail to notice it.

Two days afterward the customer came in.

"Two loafs of stale bread, if you blease.

"You haf here a fine bicture, madame," he said while she was wrapping up the bread.

"Yes?" says Miss Martha, reveling in her own cunning. "I do so admire art and" (no, it would not do to say "artists" thus early) "and paintings," she substituted. "You think it is a good picture?"

"Der balance," said the customer, "is not in good drawing. Der bairspective of it is not true. Goot morning, madame."

He took his bread, bowed, and hurried out.

Yes, he must be an artist. Miss Martha took the picture back to her room.

How gentle and kindly his eyes shone behind his spectacles! What a broad brow he had! To be able to judge perspective at a glance–and to live on stale bread! But genius often has to struggle before it is recognized.

What a thing it would be for art and perspective if genius were backed by two thousand dollars in bank, a bakery, and a sympathetic heart to– But these were day-dreams, Miss Martha.

Often now when he came he would chat for a while across the showcase.

He seemed to crave Miss Martha's cheerful words.

He kept on buying stale bread. Never a cake, never a pie, never one of her delicious Sally Lunns.

She thought he began to look thinner and discouraged. Her heart ached to add something good to eat to his meager purchase, but her courage failed at the act. She did not dare affront him. She knew the pride of artists.

Miss Martha took to wearing her blue-dotted silk waist behind the counter. In the back room she cooked a mysterious compound of quince seeds and borax. Ever so many people use it for the complexion.

One day the customer came in as usual, laid his nickel on the showcase, and called for his stale loaves. While Miss Martha was reaching for them there was a great tooting and clanging, and a fire engine came lumbering past.

The customer hurried to the door to look, as anyone will. Suddenly inspired, Miss Martha seized the opportunity.

On the bottom shelf behind the counter was a pound of fresh butter that the dairyman had left ten minutes before. With a bread knife Miss Martha made a deep slash in each of the stale loaves, inserted a generous quantity of butter, and pressed the loaves tight again.

When the customer turned once more she was tying the paper around them.

When he had gone, after an unusually pleasant little chat, Miss Martha smiled to herself, but not without a slight fluttering of the heart.

Had she been too bold? Would he take offense? But surely not. There was no language of edibles. Butter was no emblem of unmaidenly forwardness.

For a long time that day her mind dwelt on the subject. She imagined the scene when he should discover her little deception.

He would lay down his brushes and palette. There would stand his easel with the picture he was painting in which the perspective was beyond criticism.

He would prepare for his luncheon of dry bread and water. He would slice into a loaf–ah!

Miss Martha blushed. Would he think of the hand that placed it there as he ate? Would he–

The front door bell jangled viciously. Somebody was coming in, making a great deal of noise.

Miss Martha hurried to the front. Two men were there. One was a young man smoking a pipe–a man she had never seen before. The other was her artist.

His face was very red, his hat was on the back of his head, his hair was wildly rumpled. He clinched his two fists and shook them ferociously at Miss Martha. At Miss Martha.

"Dummkopf!" he shouted with extreme loudness; and then "Tausendonfer!" or something like it in German.

The young man tried to draw him away.

"I vill not go," he said angrily, "else I shall told her."

He made a bass drum of Miss Martha's counter.

"You haf shpoilt me," he cried, his blue eyes blazing behind his spectacles. "I vill tell you. You vas von meddingsome old cat!"

Miss Martha leaned weakly against the shelves and laid one hand on her blue-dotted silk waist. The young man took the other by the collar.

"Come on," he said, "you've said enough." He dragged the angry one out at the door to the sidewalk, and then came back.

"Guess you ought to be told, ma'am," he said, "what the row is about. That's Blumberger. He's an architectural draftsman. I work in the same office with him.

"He's been working hard for three months drawing a plan for a new city hall. It was a prize competition. He finished inking the lines yesterday. You know, a draftsman always makes his drawing in pencil first. When it's done he rubs out the pencil lines with handfuls of stale breadcrumbs. That's better than India rubber.

"Blumberger's been buying the bread here. Well, today–well, you know, ma'am, that butter isn't–well, Blumberger's plan isn't good for anything now except to cut up into railroad sandwiches."

Miss Martha went into the back room. She took off the blue-dotted silk waist and put on the old brown serge she used to wear. Then she poured the quince seed and borax mixture out of the window into the ash can.

The Pride *of* The Cities

aid Mr. Kipling, "The cities are full of pride, challenging each to each."
Even so.

New York was empty. Two hundred thousand of its people were away
for the summer. Three million eight hundred thousand remained as
caretakers and to pay the bills of the absentees. But the two hundred thousand are an
expensive lot.

The New Yorker sat at a roof-garden table, ingesting solace through a straw. His
panama lay upon a chair. The July audience was scattered among vacant seats as
widely as outfielders when the champion batter steps to the plate. Vaudeville
happened at intervals. The breeze was cool from the bay; around and above–
everywhere except on the stage–were stars. Glimpses were to be had of waiters,
always disappearing, like startled chamois. Prudent visitors who had ordered
refreshments by 'phone in the morning were now being served. The New Yorker was
aware of certain drawbacks to his comfort, but content beamed softly from his
rimless eyeglasses. His family was out of town. The drinks were warm; the ballet
was suffering from lack of both tune and talcum–but his family would not return
until September.

Then up into the garden stumbled the man from Topaz City, Nevada. The gloom
of the solitary sightseer enwrapped him. Bereft of joy through loneliness, he stalked
with a widower's face through the halls of pleasure. Thirst for human companionship
possessed him as he panted in the metropolitan draught. Straight to the New Yorker's
table he steered.

The New Yorker, disarmed and made reckless by the lawless atmosphere of a
roof garden, decided upon utter abandonment of his life's traditions. He resolved to
shatter with one rash, daredevil, impulsive, hair-brained act the conventions that had
hitherto been woven into his existence. Carrying out this radical and precipitous
inspiration he nodded slightly to the stranger as he drew nearer the table.

The next moment found the man from Topaz City in the list of the New Yorker's
closest friends. He took a chair at the table, he gathered two others for his feet, he
tossed his broad-brimmed hat upon a fourth, and told his life's history to his new-
found pard.

The New Yorker warmed a little, as an apartment-house furnace warms when the
strawberry season begins. A waiter who came within hail in an unguarded moment
was captured and paroled on an errand to the Doctor Wiley experimental station. The
ballet was now in the midst of a musical vagary, and danced upon the stage
programmed as Bolivian peasants, clothed in some portions of its anatomy as
Norwegian fisher maidens, in others as ladies-in-waiting of Marie Antoinette,
historically denuded in other portions so as to represent sea nymphs, and presenting
the tout ensemble of a social club of Central Park West housemaids at a fish fry.

"Been in the city long?" inquired the New Yorker, getting ready the exact tip
against the waiter's coming with large change from the bill.

"Me?" said the man from Topaz City. "Four days. Never in Topaz City, was you?"

"I!" said the New Yorker. "I was never farther west than Eighth Avenue. I had a brother who died on Ninth, but I met the cortege at Eighth. There was a bunch of violets on the hearse, and the undertaker mentioned the incident to avoid mistake. I cannot say that I am familiar with the West."

"Topaz City," said the man who occupied four chairs, "is one of the finest towns in the world."

"I presume that you have seen the sights of the metropolis," said the New Yorker, "Four days is not a sufficient length of time in which to view even our most salient points of interest, but one can possibly form a general impression. Our architectural supremacy is what generally strikes visitors to our city most forcibly. Of course you have seen our Flatiron Building. It is considered–"

"Saw it," said the man from Topaz City. "But you ought to come out our way. It's mountainous, you know, and the ladies all wear short skirts for climbing and–"

"Excuse me," said the New Yorker, "but that isn't exactly the point. New York must be a wonderful revelation to a visitor from the West. Now, as to our hotels–"

"Say," said the man from Topaz City, "that reminds me – there were sixteen stage robbers shot last year within twenty miles of –"

"I was speaking of hotels," said the New Yorker. "We lead Europe in that respect. And as far as our leisure class is concerned we are far–"

"Oh, I don't know," interrupted the man from Topaz City. "There were twelve tramps in our jail when I left home. I guess New York isn't so–"

"Beg pardon, you seem to misapprehend the idea. Of course, you visited the Stock Exchange and Wall Street, where the–"

"Oh, yes," said the man from Topaz City, as he lighted a Pennsylvania stogie, "and I want to tell you that we've got the finest town marshal west of the Rockies. Bill Rainer he took in five pickpockets out of the crowd when Red Nose Thompson laid the cornerstone of his new saloon. Topaz City don't allow…"

"Have another Rhine wine and seltzer," suggested the New Yorker. "I've never been West, as I said; but there can't be any place out there to compare with New York. As to the claims of Chicago I–"

"One man," said the Topazite–"one man only has been murdered and robbed in Topaz City in the last three–"

"Oh, I know what Chicago is," interposed the New Yorker. "Have you been up Fifth Avenue to see the magnificent residences of our mil–"

"Seen 'em all. You ought to know Reub Stegall, the assessor of Topaz. When old man Tilbury, that owns the only two-story house in town, tried to swear his taxes from $6,000 down to $450.75, Reub buckled on his forty-five and went down to see."

"Yes, yes, but speaking of our great city–one of its greatest features is our superb police department. There is no body of men in the world that can equal it for–"

"That waiter gets around like a Langley flying machine," remarked the man from Topaz City, thirstily. "We've got men in our town, too, worth $400,000. There's old Bill Withers and Colonel Metcalf and–"

"Have you seen Broadway at night?" asked the New Yorker, courteously. "There are few streets in the world that can compare with it. When the electrics are shining and the pavements are alive with two hurrying streams of elegantly clothed men and beautiful women attired in the costliest costumes that wind in and out in a close maze of expensively–"

"Never knew but one case in Topaz City," said the man from the West. "Jim Bailey, our mayor, had his watch and chain and $235 in cash taken from his pocket while–"

"That's another matter," said the New Yorker. "While you are in our city you should avail yourself of every opportunity to see its wonders. Our rapid transit system–"

"If you was out in Topaz," broke in the man from there, "I could show you a whole cemetery full of people that got killed accidentally. Talking about mangling folks up! why, when Berry Rogers turned loose that old double-barreled shot-gun of his loaded with slugs at anybody–"

"Here, waiter!" called the New Yorker. "Two more of the same. It is acknowledged by every one that our city is the center of art, and literature, and learning. Take, for instance, our after-dinner speakers. Where else in the country would you find such wit and eloquence as emanate from Depew and Ford, and–"

"If you take the papers," interrupted the Westerner, "you must have read of Pete Webster's daughter. The Websters live two blocks north of the courthouse in Topaz City. Miss Tillie Webster, she slept forty days and nights without waking up. The doctors said that–"

"Pass the matches, please," said the New Yorker. "Have you observed the expedition with which new buildings are being run up in New York? Improved inventions in steel framework and–"

"I noticed," said the Nevadian, "that the statistics of Topaz City showed only one carpenter crushed by falling timbers last year and he was caught in a cyclone."

"They abuse our sky line," continued the New Yorker, "and it is likely that we are not yet artistic in the construction of our buildings. But I can safely assert that we lead in pictorial and decorative art. In some of our houses can be found masterpieces in the way of paintings and sculpture. One who has the entree to our best galleries will find–"

"Back up," exclaimed the man from Topaz City. "There was a game last month in our town in which $90,000 changed hands on a pair of–"

"Ta-romt-tara!" went the orchestra. The stage curtain, blushing pink at the name "Asbestos" inscribed upon it, came down with a slow midsummer movement. The audience trickled leisurely down the elevator and stairs.

On the sidewalk below, the New Yorker and the man from Topaz City shook hands with alcoholic gravity. The elevated crashed raucously, surface cars hummed and clanged, cabmen swore, newsboys shrieked, wheels clattered ear-piercingly. The New Yorker conceived a happy thought, with which he aspired to clinch the pre-eminence of his city.

"You must admit," said he, "that in the way of noise New York is far ahead of any other–"

"Back to the everglades!" said the man from Topaz City. "In 1900, when Sousa's band and the repeating candidate were in our town you couldn't–"

The rattle of an express wagon drowned the rest of the words.

Holding Up A Train

Note. The man who told me these things was for several years an outlaw in the Southwest and a follower of the pursuit he so frankly describes. His description of the modus operandi should prove interesting, his counsel of value to the potential passenger in some future "hold-up," while his estimate of the pleasures of train robbing will hardly induce any one to adopt it as a profession. I give the story in almost exactly his own words. O. H.

ost people would say, if their opinion was asked for, that holding up a train would be a hard job. Well, it isn't; it's easy. I have contributed some to the uneasiness of railroads and the insomnia of express companies, and the most trouble I ever had about a hold-up was in being swindled by unscrupulous people while spending the money I got. The danger wasn't anything to speak of, and we didn't mind the trouble.

One man has come pretty near robbing a train by himself; two have succeeded a few times; three can do it if they are hustlers, but five is about the right number. The time to do it and the place depend upon several things.

The first "stick-up" I was ever in happened in 1890. Maybe the way I got into it will explain how most train robbers start in the business. Five out of six Western outlaws are just cowboys out of a job and gone wrong. The sixth is a tough from the East who dresses up like a bad man and plays some low-down trick that gives the boys a bad name. Wire fences and "nesters" made five of them; a bad heart made the sixth.

Jim S— and I were working on the 101 Ranch in Colorado. The nesters had the cowman on the go. They had taken up the land and elected officers who were hard to get along with. Jim and I rode into La Junta one day, going south from a round-up. We were having a little fun without malice toward anybody when a farmer administration cut in and tried to harvest us. Jim shot a deputy marshal, and I kind of corroborated his side of the argument. We skirmished up and down the main street, the boomers having bad luck all the time. After a while we leaned forward and shoved for the ranch down on the Ceriso. We were riding a couple of horses that couldn't fly, but they could catch birds.

A few days after that, a gang of the La Junta boomers came to the ranch and wanted us to go back with them. Naturally, we declined. We had the house on them, and before we were done refusing, that old 'dobe was plumb full of lead. When dark came we fagged 'em a batch of bullets and shoved out the back door for the rocks. They sure smoked us as we went. We had to drift, which we did, and rounded up down in Oklahoma.

Well, there wasn't anything we could get there, and, being mighty hard up, we decided to transact a little business with the railroads. Jim and I joined forces with Tom and Ike Moore–two brothers who had plenty of sand they were willing to convert into dust. I can call their names, for both of them are dead. Tom was shot while robbing a bank in Arkansas; Ike was killed during the more dangerous pastime of attending a dance in the Creek Nation.

We selected a place on the Santa Fe where there was a bridge across a deep creek surrounded by heavy timber. All passenger trains took water at the tank close to one end of the bridge. It was a quiet place, the nearest house being five miles away. The day before it happened, we rested our horses and "made medicine" as to how we should get about it. Our plans were not at all elaborate, as none of us had ever engaged in a hold-up before.

The Santa Fe flyer was due at the tank at 11.15 P. M. At eleven, Tom and I lay down on one side of the track, and Jim and Ike took the other. As the train rolled up, the headlight flashing far down the track and the steam hissing from the engine, I turned weak all over. I would have worked a whole year on the ranch for nothing to have been out of that affair right then. Some of the nerviest men in the business have told me that they felt the same way the first time.

The engine had hardly stopped when I jumped on the running-board on one side, while Jim mounted the other. As soon as the engineer and fireman saw our guns they threw up their hands without being told, and begged us not to shoot, saying they would do anything we wanted them to.

"Hit the ground," I ordered, and they both jumped off. We drove them before us down the side of the train. While this was happening, Tom and Ike had been blazing away, one on each side of the train, yelling like Apaches, so as to keep the passengers herded in the cars. Some fellow stuck a little twenty-two caliber out one of the coach windows and fired it straight up in the air. I let drive and smashed the glass just over his head. That settled everything like resistance from that direction.

By this time all my nervousness was gone. I felt a kind of pleasant excitement as if I were at a dance or a frolic of some sort. The lights were all out in the coaches, and, as Tom and Ike gradually quit firing and yelling, it got to be almost as still as a graveyard. I remember hearing a little bird chirping in a bush at the side of the track, as if it were complaining at being waked up.

I made the fireman get a lantern, and then I went to the express car and yelled to the messenger to open up or get perforated. He slid the door back and stood in it with his hands up. "Jump overboard, son," I said, and he hit the dirt like a lump of lead. There were two safes in the car–a big one and a little one. By the way, I first located the messenger's arsenal–a double-barreled shotgun with buckshot cartridges and a thirty-eight in a drawer. I drew the cartridges from the shotgun, pocketed the pistol, and called the messenger inside. I shoved my gun against his nose and put him to work. He couldn't open the big safe, but he did the little one. There was only nine hundred dollars in it. That was mighty small winnings for our trouble, so we decided to go through the passengers. We took our prisoners to the smoking-car, and from there sent the engineer through the train to light up the coaches. Beginning with the first one, we placed a man at each door and ordered the passengers to stand between the seats with their hands up.

If you want to find out what cowards the majority of men are, all you have to do is rob a passenger train. I don't mean because they don't resist–I'll tell you later on why they can't do that–but it makes a man feel sorry for them the way they lose their heads. Big, burly drummers and farmers and ex-soldiers and high-collared dudes and sports that, a few moments before, were filling the car with noise and bragging, get so scared that their ears flop.

There were very few people in the day coaches at that time of night, so we made a slim haul until we got to the sleeper. The Pullman conductor met me at one door while Jim was going round to the other one. He very politely informed me that I could not go into that car, as it did not belong to the railroad company, and, besides, the passengers had already been greatly disturbed by the shouting and firing. Never in all my life have I met with a finer instance of official dignity and reliance upon the power of Mr. Pullman's great name. I jabbed my six-shooter so hard against Mr. Conductor's front that I afterward found one of his vest buttons so firmly wedged in the end of the barrel that I had to shoot it out. He just shut up like a weak-springed knife and rolled down the car steps.

I opened the door of the sleeper and stepped inside. A big, fat old man came wabbling up to me, puffing and blowing. He had one coat-sleeve on and was trying to put his vest on over that. I don't know who he thought I was.

"Young man, young man," says he, "you must keep cool and not get excited. Above everything, keep cool."

"I can't," says I. "Excitement's just eating me up." And then I let out a yell and turned loose my forty-five through the skylight.

That old man tried to dive into one of the lower berths, but a screech came out of it and a bare foot that took him in the breadbasket and landed him on the floor. I saw Jim coming in the other door, and I hollered for everybody to climb out and line up.

They commenced to scramble down, and for a while we had a three-ringed circus. The men looked as frightened and tame as a lot of rabbits in a deep snow. They had on, on an average, about a quarter of a suit of clothes and one shoe apiece. One chap was sitting on the floor of the aisle, looking as if he were working a hard sum in arithmetic. He was trying, very solemn, to pull a lady's number two shoe on his number nine foot.

The ladies didn't stop to dress. They were so curious to see a real, live train robber, bless 'em, that they just wrapped blankets and sheets around themselves and came out, squeaky and fidgety looking. They always show more curiosity and sand than the men do.

We got them all lined up and pretty quiet, and I went through the bunch. I found very little on them—I mean in the way of valuables. One man in the line was a sight. He was one of those big, overgrown, solemn snoozers that sit on the platform at lectures and look wise. Before crawling out he had managed to put on his long, frock-tailed coat and his high silk hat. The rest of him was nothing but pajamas and bunions. When I dug into that Prince Albert, I expected to drag out at least a block of gold mine stock or an armful of Government bonds, but all I found was a little boy's French harp about four inches long. What it was there for, I don't know. I felt a little mad because he had fooled me so. I stuck the harp up against his mouth.

"If you can't pay—play," I says.

"I can't play," says he.

"Then learn right off quick," says I, letting him smell the end of my gun-barrel.

He caught hold of the harp, turned red as a beet, and commenced to blow. He blew a dinky little tune I remembered hearing when I was a kid:

Prettiest little gal in the country—oh!
Mammy and Daddy told me so.

I made him keep on playing it all the time we were in the car. Now and then he'd get weak and off the key, and I'd turn my gun on him and ask what was the matter with that little gal, and whether he had any intention of going back on her, which would make him start up again like sixty. I think that old boy standing there in his silk hat and bare feet, playing his little French harp, was the funniest sight I ever saw. One little redheaded woman in the line broke out laughing at him. You could have heard her in the next car.

Then Jim held them steady while I searched the berths. I grappled around in those beds and filled a pillowcase with the strangest assortment of stuff you ever saw. Now and then I'd come across a little popgun pistol, just about right for plugging teeth with, which I'd throw out the window. When I finished with the collection, I dumped the pillowcase load in the middle of the aisle. There were a good many watches, bracelets, rings, and pocket books, with a sprinkling of false teeth, whiskey flasks, face-powder boxes, chocolate caramels, and heads of hair of various colors and lengths. There were also about a dozen ladies' stockings into which jewelry, watches, and rolls of bills had been stuffed and then wadded up tight and stuck under the mattresses. I offered to return what I called the "scalps," saying that we were not Indians on the warpath, but none of the ladies seemed to know to whom the hair belonged.

One of the women--and a good-looker she was--wrapped in a striped blanket, saw me pick up one of the stockings that was pretty chunky and heavy about the toe, and she snapped out:

"That's mine, sir. You're not in the business of robbing women, are you?"

Now, as this was our first hold-up, we hadn't agreed upon any code of ethics, so I hardly knew what to answer. But, anyway, I replied: "Well, not as a specialty. If this contains your personal property you can have it back."

"It just does," she declared eagerly, and reached out her hand for it.

"You'll excuse my taking a look at the contents," I said, holding the stocking up by the toe. Out dumped a big gent's gold watch, worth two hundred, a gent's leather pocket-book that we afterward found to contain six hundred dollars, a 32-calibre revolver; and the only thing of the lot that could have been a lady's personal property was a silver bracelet worth about fifty cents.

I said: "Madame, here's your property," and handed her the bracelet. "Now," I went on, "how can you expect us to act square with you when you try to deceive us in this manner? I'm surprised at such conduct."

The young woman flushed up as if she had been caught doing something dishonest. Some other woman down the line called out: "The mean thing!" I never knew whether she meant the other lady or me.

When we finished our job we ordered everybody back to bed, told 'em good night very politely at the door, and left. We rode forty miles before daylight and then divided the stuff. Each one of us got $1,752.85 in money. We lumped the jewelry around. Then we scattered, each man for himself.

That was my first train robbery, and it was about as easily done as any of the ones that followed. But that was the last and only time I ever went through the passengers. I don't like that part of the business. Afterward I stuck strictly to the express car. During the next eight years I handled a good deal of money.

The best haul I made was just seven years after the first one. We found out about a train that was going to bring out a lot of money to pay off the soldiers at a Government post. We stuck that train up in broad daylight. Five of us lay in the sand hills near a little station. Ten soldiers were guarding the money on the train, but they might just as well have been at home on a furlough. We didn't even allow them to stick their heads out the windows to see the fun. We had no trouble at all in getting the money, which was all in gold. Of course, a big howl was raised at the time about the robbery. It was Government stuff, and the Government got sarcastic and wanted to know what the convoy of soldiers went along for. The only excuse given was that nobody was expecting an attack among those bare sand hills in daytime. I don't know what the Government thought about the excuse, but I know that it was a good one. The surprise—that is the keynote of the train-robbing business. The papers published all kinds of stories about the loss, finally agreeing that it was between nine thousand and ten thousand dollars. The Government sawed wood. Here are the correct figures, printed for the first time—forty-eight thousand dollars. If anybody will take the trouble to look over Uncle Sam's private accounts for that little debit to profit and loss, he will find that I am right to a cent.

By that time we were expert enough to know what to do. We rode due west twenty miles, making a trail that a Broadway policeman could have followed, and then we doubled back, hiding our tracks. On the second night after the hold-up, while posses were scouring the country in every direction, Jim and I were eating supper in the second story of a friend's house in the town where the alarm started from. Our friend pointed out to us, in an office across the street, a printing press at work striking off handbills offering a reward for our capture.

I have been asked what we do with the money we get. Well, I never could account for a tenth part of it after it was spent. It goes fast and freely. An outlaw has to have a good many friends. A highly respected citizen may, and often does, get along with very few, but a man on the dodge has got to have "sidekickers." With angry posses and reward-hungry officers cutting out a hot trail for him, he must have a few places scattered about the country where he can stop and feed himself and his horse and get a few hours' sleep without having to keep both eyes open. When he makes a haul he feels like dropping some of the coin with these friends, and he does it liberally. Sometimes I have, at the end of a hasty visit at one of these havens of refuge, flung a handful of gold and bills into the laps of the kids playing on the floor, without knowing whether my contribution was a hundred dollars or a thousand.

When old-timers make a big haul they generally go far away to one of the big cities to spend their money. Green hands, however successful a hold-up they make, nearly always give themselves away by showing too much money near the place where they got it.

I was in a job in '94 where we got twenty thousand dollars. We followed our favorite plan for a get-away—that is, doubled on our trail—and laid low for a time near the scene of the train's bad luck. One morning I picked up a newspaper and read an article with big headlines stating that the marshal, with eight deputies and a posse of thirty armed citizens, had the train robbers surrounded in a mesquite thicket on the Cimarron, and that it was a question of only a few hours when they would be dead men or prisoners. While I was reading that article I was sitting at breakfast in one of the most elegant private residences in Washington City, with a flunky in knee pants standing behind my chair. Jim was sitting across the table talking to his half-uncle, a retired naval officer, whose name you have often seen in the accounts of doings in the capital. We had gone there and bought rattling outfits of good clothes, and were resting from our labors among the nabobs. We must have been killed in that mesquite thicket, for I can make an affidavit that we didn'tsurrender.

Now I propose to tell why it is easy to hold up a train, and, then, why no one should ever do it.

In the first place, the attacking party has all the advantage. That is, of course, supposing that they are old-timers with the necessary experience and courage. They have the outside and are protected by the darkness, while the others are in the light, hemmed into a small space, and exposed, the moment they show a head at a window or door, to the aim of a man who is a dead shot and who won't hesitate to shoot.

But, in my opinion, the main condition that makes train robbing easy is the element of surprise in connection with the imagination of the passengers. If you have ever seen a horse that has eaten locoweed you will understand what I mean when I say that the passengers get locoed. That horse gets the awfullest imagination on him in the world. You can't coax him to cross a little branch stream two feet wide. It looks as big to him as the Mississippi River. That's just the way with the passenger. He thinks there are a hundred men yelling and shooting outside, when maybe there are only two or three. And the muzzle of a forty-five looks like the entrance to a tunnel. The passenger is all right, although he may do mean little tricks, like hiding a wad of money in his shoe and forgetting to dig-up until you jostle his ribs some with the end of your six-shooter; but there's no harm in him.

As to the train crew, we never had any more trouble with them than if they had been so many sheep. I don't mean that they are cowards; I mean that they have got sense. They know they're not up against a bluff. It's the same way with the officers. I've seen secret service men, marshals, and railroad detectives fork over their change as meek as Moses. I saw one of the bravest marshals I ever knew hide his gun under his seat and dig up along with the rest while I was taking toll. He wasn't afraid; he simply knew that we had the drop on the whole outfit. Besides, many of those officers have families and they feel that they oughtn't to take chances; whereas death has no terrors for the man who holds up a train. He expects to get killed some day, and he generally does. My advice to you, if you should ever be in a hold-up, is to line up with the cowards and save your bravery for an occasion when it may be of some benefit to you. Another reason why officers are backward about mixing things with a train robber is a financial one. Every time there is a scrimmage and somebody gets killed, the officers lose money. If the train robber gets away they swear out a warrant against John Doe *et al.* and travel hundreds of miles and sign vouchers for thousands on the trail of the fugitives, and the Government foots the bills. So, with them, it is a question of mileage rather than courage.

I will give one instance to support my statement that the surprise is the best card in playing for a hold-up.

Along in '92 the Daltons were cutting out a hot trail for the officers down in the Cherokee Nation, those were their lucky days, and they got so reckless and sandy, that they used to announce beforehand what job they were going to undertake. Once they gave it out that they were going to hold up the M. K. & T. flyer on a certain night at the station of Pryor Creek, in Indian Territory.

That night the railroad company got fifteen deputy marshals in Muscogee and put them on the train. Beside them they had fifty armed men hid in the depot at Pryor Creek.

When the Katy Flyer pulled in not a Dalton showed up. The next station was Adair, six miles away. When the train reached there, and the deputies were having a good time explaining what they would have done to the Dalton gang if they had turned up, all at once it sounded like an army firing outside. The conductor and brakeman came running into the car yelling, "Trainrobbers!"

Some of those deputies lit out of the door, hit the ground, and kept on running. Some of them hid their Winchesters under the seats. Two of them made a fight and were both killed.

It took the Daltons just ten minutes to capture the train and whip the escort. In twenty minutes more they robbed the express car of twenty-seven thousand dollars and made a clean get-away.

My opinion is that those deputies would have put up a stiff fight at Pryor Creek, where they were expecting trouble, but they were taken by surprise and "locoed" at Adair, just as the Daltons, who knew their business, expected they would.

I don't think I ought to close without giving some deductions from my experience of eight years "on the dodge." It doesn't pay to rob trains. Leaving out the question of right and morals, which I don't think I ought to tackle, there is very little to envy in the life of an outlaw. After a while money ceases to have any value in his eyes. He gets to looking upon the railroads and express companies as his bankers, and his six-shooter as a cheque book good for any amount. He throws away money right and left. Most of the time he is on the jump, riding day and night, and he lives so hard between times that he doesn't enjoy the taste of high life when he gets it. He knows that his time is bound to come to lose his life or liberty, and that the accuracy of his aim, the speed of his horse, and the fidelity of his "sider," are all that postpone the inevitable.

It isn't that he loses any sleep over danger from the officers of the law. In all my experience I never knew officers to attack a band of outlaws unless they outnumbered them at least three to one.

But the outlaw carries one thought constantly in his mind—and that is what makes him so sore against life, more than anything else—he knows where the marshals get their recruits of deputies. He knows that the majority of these upholders of the law were once lawbreakers, horse thieves, rustlers, highwaymen, and outlaws like himself, and that they gained their positions and immunity by turning state's evidence, by turning traitor and delivering up their comrades to imprisonment and death. He knows that someday—unless he is shot first—his Judas will set to work, the trap will be laid, and he will be the surprised instead of a surpriser at a stick-up.

That is why the man who holds up trains picks his company with a thousand times the care with which a careful girl chooses a sweetheart. That is why he raises himself from his blanket of nights and listens to the tread of every horse's hoofs on the distant road. That is why he broods suspiciously for days upon a jesting remark or an unusual movement of a tried comrade, or the broken mutterings of his closest friend, sleeping by his side.

And it is one of the reasons why the train-robbing profession is not so pleasant a one as either of its collateral branches—politics or cornering the market.

Ulysses *and the* Dogman

o you know the time of the dogmen?

When the forefinger of twilight begins to smudge the clear-drawn lines of the Big City there is inaugurated an hour devoted to one of the most melancholy sights of urban life.

Out from the towering flat crags and apartment peaks of the cliff dwellers of New York steals an army of beings that were once men. Even yet they go upright upon two limbs and retain human form and speech; but you will observe that they are behind animals in progress. Each of these beings follows a dog, to which he is fastened by an artificial ligament.

These men are all victims to Circe. Not willingly do they become flunkeys to Fido, bell boys to bull terriers, and toddlers after Towzer. Modern Circe, instead of turning them into animals, has kindly left the difference of a six-foot leash between them. Every one of those dogmen has been either cajoled, bribed, or commanded by his own particular Circe to take the dear household pet out for an airing.

By their faces and manner you can tell that the dogmen are bound in a hopeless enchantment. Never will there come even a dogcatcher Ulysses to remove the spell.

The faces of some are stonily set. They are past the commiseration, the curiosity, or the jeers of their fellow-beings. Years of matrimony, of continuous compulsory canine constitutionals, have made them callous. They unwind their beasts from lampposts, or the ensnared legs of profane pedestrians, with the stolidity of mandarins manipulating the strings of their kites.

Others, more recently reduced to the ranks of Rover's retinue, take their medicine sulkily and fiercely. They play the dog on the end of their line with the pleasure felt by the girl out fishing when she catches a sea-robin on her hook. They glare at you threateningly if you look at them, as if it would be their delight to let slip the dogs of war. These are half-mutinous dogmen, not quite Circe-ized, and you will do well not to kick their charges, should they sniff around your ankles.

Others of the tribe do not seem to feel so keenly. They are mostly unfresh youths, with gold caps and drooping cigarettes, who do not harmonize with their dogs. The animals they attend wear satin bows in their collars; and the young men steer them so assiduously that you are tempted to the theory that some personal advantage, contingent upon satisfactory service, waits upon the execution of their duties.

The dogs thus personally conducted are of many varieties; but they are one in fatness, in pampered, diseased vileness of temper, in insolent, snarling capriciousness of behavior. They tug at the leash fractiously, they make leisurely nasal inventory of every doorstep, railing, and post. They sit down to rest when they choose; they wheeze like the winner of a Third Avenue beefsteak-eating contest; they blunder clumsily into open cellars and coal holes; they lead the dogmen a merry dance.

These unfortunate dry nurses of dogdom, the cur cuddlers, mongrel managers, Spitz stalkers, poodle pullers, Skye scrapers, dachshund dandlers, terrier trailers and Pomeranian pushers of the cliff-dwelling Circes follow their charges meekly. The doggies neither fear nor respect them. Masters of the house these men whom they hold in leash may be, but they are not masters of them. From cozy corner to fire escape, from divan to dumbwaiter, doggy's snarl easily drives this two-legged being who is commissioned to walk at the other end of his string during his outing.

One twilight the dogmen came forth as usual at their Circes' pleading, guerdon, or crack of the whip. One among them was a strong man, apparently of too solid virtues for this airy vocation. His expression was melancholic, his manner depressed. He was leashed to a vile white dog, loathsomely fat, fiendishly ill-natured, gloatingly intractable toward his despised conductor.

At a corner nearest to his apartment house the dogman turned down a side street, hoping for fewer witnesses to his ignominy. The surfeited beast waddled before him, panting with spleen and the labor of motion.

Suddenly the dog stopped. A tall, brown, long-coated, wide-brimmed man stood like a Colossus blocking the sidewalk and declaring:

"Well, I'm a son of a gun!"

"Jim Berry!" breathed the dogman, with exclamation points in his voice.

"Sam Telfair," cried Wide-Brim again, "you ding-basted old willy-walloo, give us your hoof!"

Their hands clasped in the brief, tight greeting of the West that is death to the handshake microbe.

"You old fat rascal!" continued Wide-Brim, with a wrinkled brown smile; "it's been five years since I seen you. I been in this town a week, but you can't find nobody in such a place. Well, you dinged old married man, how are they coming?"

Something mushy and heavily soft like raised dough leaned against Jim's leg and chewed his trousers with a yeasty growl.

"Get to work," said Jim, "and explain this yard-wide hydrophobia yearling you've throwed your lasso over. Are you the pound-master of this burg? Do you call that a dog or what?"

"I need a drink," said the dogman, dejected at the reminder of his old dog of the sea. "Come on."

Hard by was a cafe. 'Tis ever so in the big city.

They sat at a table, and the bloated monster yelped and scrambled at the end of his leash to get at the cafe cat.

"Whiskey," said Jim to the waiter. "Make it two," said the dogman.

"You're fatter," said Jim, "and you look subjugated. I don't know about the East agreeing with you. All the boys asked me to hunt you up when I started. Sandy King, he went to the Klondike. Watson Burrel, he married the oldest Peters girl. I made some money buying beeves, and I bought a lot of wild land up on the Little Powder. Going to fence next fall. Bill Rawlins, he's gone to farming. You remember Bill, of course–he was courting Marcella– excuse me, Sam–I mean the lady you married, while she was teaching school at Prairie View. But you was the lucky man. How is Missis Telfair?"

"S-h-h-h!" said the dogman, signaling the waiter; "give it a name."

"Whiskey," said Jim.

"Make it two," said the dogman.

"She's well," he continued, after his chaser. "She refused to live anywhere but in New York, where she came from. We live in a flat. Every evening at six I take that dog out for a walk. It's Marcella's pet. There never were two animals on earth, Jim, that hated one another like me and that dog does. His name's Lovekins. Marcella dresses for dinner while we're out. We eat tabble dote. Ever try one of them, Jim?"

"No, I never," said Jim. "I seen the signs, but I thought they said 'table de hole.' I thought it was French for pool tables. How does it taste?"

"If you're going to be in the city for a while we will—"

"No, sir-ee. I'm starting for home this evening on the 7:25. Like to stay longer, but I can't."

"I'll walk down to the ferry with you," said the dogman.

The dog had bound a leg each of Jim and the chair together, and had sunk into a comatose slumber. Jim stumbled, and the leash was slightly wrenched. The shrieks of the awakened beast rang for a block around.

"If that's your dog," said Jim, when they were on the street again, "what's to hinder you from running that habeas corpus you've got around his neck over a limb and walking off and forgetting him?"

"I'd never dare to," said the dogman, awed at the bold proposition. "He sleeps in the bed, I sleep on a lounge. He runs howling to Marcella if I look at him. Some night, Jim, I'm going to get even with that dog. I've made up my mind to do it. I'm going to creep over with a knife and cut a hole in his mosquito bar so they can get in to him. See if I don't do it!"

"You ain't yourself, Sam Telfair. You ain't what you was once. I don't know about these cities and flats over here. With my own eyes I seen you stand off both the Tillotson boys in Prairie View with the brass faucet out of a molasses barrel. And I seen you rope and tie the wildest steer on Little Powder in 39 1-2."

"I did, didn't I?" said the other, with a temporary gleam in his eye. "But that was before I was dogmatized."

"Does Misses Telfair—" began Jim.

"Hush!" said the dogman. "Here's another cafe."

They lined up at the bar. The dog fell asleep at their feet.

"Whiskey," said Jim.

"Make it two," said the dogman.

"I thought about you," said Jim, "when I bought that wild land. I wished you was out there to help me with the stock."

"Last Tuesday," said the dogman, "he bit me on the ankle because I asked for cream in my coffee. He always gets the cream."

"You'd like Prairie View now," said Jim. "The boys from the round-ups for fifty miles around ride in there. One corner of my pasture is in sixteen miles of the town. There's a straight forty miles of wire on one side of it."

"You pass through the kitchen to get to the bedroom," said the dogman, "and you pass through the parlor to get to the bath room, and you back out through the dining-room to get into the bedroom so you can turn around and leave by the kitchen. And he snores and barks in his sleep, and I have to smoke in the park on account of his asthma."

"Don't Missis Telfair—" began Jim.

"Oh, shut up!" said the dogman. "What is it this time?"

"Whiskey," said Jim.

"Make it two," said the dogman.

"Well, I'll be racking along down toward the ferry," said the other.

"Come on, there, you mangy, turtle-backed, snake-headed, bench-legged ton-and-a-half of soap-grease!" shouted the dogman, with a new note in his voice and a new hand on the leash. The dog scrambled after them, with an angry whine at such unusual language from his guardian.

At the foot of Twenty-third Street the dogman led the way through swinging doors.

"Last chance," said he. "Speak up."

"Whiskey," said Jim.

"Make it two," said the dogman.

"I don't know," said the ranchman, "where I'll find the man I want to take charge of the Little Powder outfit. I want somebody I know something about. Finest stretch of prairie and timber you ever squinted your eye over, Sam. Now if you was–"

"Speaking of hydrophobia," said the dogman, "the other night he chewed a piece out of my leg because I knocked a fly off of Marcella's arm. 'It ought to be cauterized,' says Marcella, and I was thinking so myself. I telephones for the doctor, and when he comes Marcella says to me: 'Help me hold the poor dear while the doctor fixes his mouth. Oh, I hope he got no virus on any of his toofies when he bit you.' Now what do you think of that?"

"Does Missis Telfair–" began Jim.

"Oh, drop it," said the dogman. "Come again."

"Whiskey," said Jim.

"Make it two," said the dogman.

They walked on to the ferry. The ranchman stepped to the ticket window. Suddenly the swift landing of three or four heavy kicks was heard, the air was rent by piercing canine shrieks, and a pained, outraged, lubberly, bow-legged pudding of a dog ran frenziedly up the street alone.

"Ticket to Denver," said Jim.

"Make it two," shouted the ex-dogman, reaching for his inside pocket.

The Champion *of the* Weather

f you should speak of the Kiowa Reservation to the average New Yorker, he probably wouldn't know whether you were referring to a new political dodge at Albany or a leitmotif from "Parsifal." But out in the Kiowa Reservation advices have been received concerning the existence of New York.

A party of us were on a hunting trip in the Reservation. Bud Kingsbury, our guide, philosopher, and friend, was broiling antelope steaks in camp one night. One of the party, a pinkish-haired young man in a correct hunting costume, sauntered over to the fire to light a cigarette, and remarked carelessly to Bud:

"Nice night!"

"Why, yes," said Bud, "as nice as any night could be that ain't received the Broadway stamp of approval."

Now, the young man was from New York, but the rest of us wondered how Bud guessed it. So, when the steaks were done, we besought him to lay bare his system of ratiocination. And as Bud was something of a Territorial talking machine he made oration as follows:

"How did I know he was from New York? Well, I figured it out as soon as he sprung them two words on me. I was in New York myself a couple of years ago, and I noticed some of the earmarks and hoof tracks of the Rancho Manhattan."

"Found New York rather different from the Panhandle, didn't you, Bud?" asked one of the hunters.

"Can't say that I did," answered Bud; "anyways, not more than some. The main trail in that town which they call Broadway is plenty traveled, but they're about the same brand of bipeds that tramp around in Cheyenne and Amarillo, At first I was sort of rattled by the crowds, but I soon says to myself, 'Here, now, Bud; they're just plain folks like you and Geronimo and Grover Cleveland and the Watson boys, so don't get all flustered up with consternation under your saddle blanket,' and then I feels calm and peaceful, like I was back in the Nation again at a ghost dance or a green corn pow-wow.

"I'd been saving up for a year to give this New York a whirl. I knew a man named Summers that lived there, but I couldn't find him; so I played a lone hand at enjoying the intoxicating pleasures of the corn-fed metropolis.

"For a while I was so frivolous and locoed by the electric lights and the noises of the phonographs and the second-story railroads that I forgot one of the crying needs of my Western system of natural requirements. I never was no hand to deny myself the pleasures of sociable vocal intercourse with friends and strangers. Out in the Territories when I meet a man I never saw before, inside of nine minutes I know his income, religion, size of collar, and his wife's temper, and how much he pays for clothes, alimony, and chewing tobacco. It's a gift with me not to be penurious with my conversation.

"But this here New York was inaugurated on the idea of abstemiousness in regard to the parts of speech. At the end of three weeks nobody in the city had fired even a blank syllable in my direction except the waiter in the grub emporium where I fed. And as his outpourings of syntax wasn't nothing but plagiarisms from the bill of fare, he never satisfied my yearnings, which was to have somebody hit. If I stood next to a man at a bar he'd edge off and give a Baldwin-Ziegler look as if he suspected me of having the North Pole concealed on my person. I began to wish that I'd gone to Abilene or Waco for my *paseado*; for the mayor of them places will drink with you, and the first citizen you meet will tell you his middle name and ask you to take a chance in a raffle for a music box.

"Well, one day when I was particular hankering for to be gregarious with something more loquacious than a lamp post, a fellow in a caffy says to me, says he:

"'Nice day!'

"He was a kind of a manager of the place, and I reckon he'd seen me in there a good many times. He had a face like a fish and an eye like Judas, but I got up and put one arm around his neck.

"'Pardner,' I says, 'sure it's a nice day. You're the first gentleman in all New York to observe that the intricacies of human speech might not be altogether wasted on William Kingsbury. But don't you think,' says I, 'that 'twas a little cool early in the morning; and ain't there a feeling of rain in the air tonight? But along about noon it sure was gallupsious weather. How's all up to the house? You doing right well with the caffy, now?'

"Well, sir, that galoot just turns his back and walks off stiff, without a word, after all my trying to be agreeable! I didn't know what to make of it. That night I finds a note from Summers, who'd been away from town, giving the address of his camp. I goes up to his house and has a good, old-time talk with his folks. And I tells Summers about the actions of this coyote in the caffy, and desires interpretation.

"'Oh,' says Summers, 'he wasn't intending to strike up a conversation with you. That's just the New York style. He'd seen you was a regular customer and he spoke a word or two just to show you he appreciated your custom. You oughtn't to have followed it up. That's about as far as we care to go with a stranger. A word or so about the weather may be ventured, but we don't generally make it the basis of an acquaintance.'

"'Billy,' says I, 'the weather and its ramifications is a solemn subject with me. Meteorology is one of my sore points. No man can open up the question of temperature or humidity or the glad sunshine with me, and then turn tail on it without its leading to a falling barometer. I'm going down to see that man again and give him a lesson in the art of continuous conversation. You say New York etiquette allows him two words and no answer. Well, he's going to turn himself into a weather bureau and finish what he begun with me, besides indulging in neighborly remarks on other subjects.'

"Summers talked agin it, but I was irritated some and I went on the street car back to that caffy.

"The same fellow was there yet, walking round in a sort of back corral where there was tables and chairs. A few people was sitting around having drinks and sneering at one another.

"I called that man to one side and herded him into a corner. I unbuttoned enough to show him a thirty-eight I carried stuck under my vest.

"'Pardner,' I says, 'a brief space ago I was in here and you seized the opportunity to say it was a nice day. When I attempted to corroborate your weather signal, you turned your back and walked off. Now,' says I, 'you frog-hearted, language-shy, stiff-necked cross between a Spitzbergen sea cook and a muzzled oyster, you resume where you left off in your discourse on the weather.'

"The fellow looks at me and tries to grin, but he sees I don't and he comes around serious.

"'Well,' says he, eyeing the handle of my gun, 'it was rather a nice day; some warmish, though.'

"'Particulars, you mealy-mouthed snoozer,' I says, 'let's have the specifications–expatiate–fill in the outlines. When you start anything with me in short-hand it's bound to turn out a storm signal.'

"'Looked like rain yesterday,' says the man, 'but it cleared off fine in the forenoon. I hear the farmers are needing rain right badly up-State.'

"'That's the kind of a canter,' says I. 'Shake the New York dust off your hoofs and be a real agreeable kind of a centaur. You broke the ice, you know, and we're getting better acquainted every minute. Seems to me I asked you about your family?'

"'They're all well, thanks,' says he. 'We—we have a new piano.'

"'Now you're coming it,' I says. 'This cold reserve is breaking up at last. That little touch about the piano almost makes us brothers. What's the youngest kid's name?' I asks him.

"'Thomas,' says he. 'He's just getting well from the measles.'

"'I feel like I'd known you always,' says I. 'Now there was just one more– are you doing right well with the caffy, now?'

"'Pretty well,' he says. 'I'm putting away a little money.'

"'Glad to hear it,' says I. 'Now go back to your work and get civilized. Keep your hands off the weather unless you're ready to follow it up in a personal manner, It's a subject that naturally belongs to sociability and the forming of new ties, and I hate to see it handed out in small change in a town like this.'

"So the next day I rolls up my blankets and hits the trail away from New York City."

For many minutes after Bud ceased talking we lingered around the fire, and then all hands began to disperse for bed.

As I was unrolling my bedding I heard the pinkish-haired young man saying to Bud, with something like anxiety in his voice:

"As I say, Mr. Kingsbury, there is something really beautiful about this night. The delightful breeze and the bright stars and the clear air unite in making it wonderfully attractive."

"Yes," said Bud, "it's a nice night."

Makes *the* Whole World Kin

he burglar stepped inside the window quickly, and then he took his time. A burglar who respects his art always takes his time before taking anything else.

The house was a private residence. By its boarded front door and untrimmed Boston ivy the burglar knew that the mistress of it was sitting on some oceanside piazza telling a sympathetic man in a yachting cap that no one had ever understood her sensitive, lonely heart. He knew by the light in the third-story front windows, and by the lateness of the season, that the master of the house had come home, and would soon extinguish his light and retire. For it was September of the year and of the soul, in which season the house's good man comes to consider roof gardens and stenographers as vanities, and to desire the return of his mate and the more durable blessings of decorum and the moral excellencies.

The burglar lighted a cigarette. The guarded glow of the match illuminated his salient points for a moment. He belonged to the third type of burglars.

This third type has not yet been recognized and accepted. The police have made us familiar with the first and second. Their classification is simple. The collar is the distinguishing mark.

When a burglar is caught who does not wear a collar he is described as a degenerate of the lowest type, singularly vicious and depraved, and is suspected of being the desperate criminal who stole the handcuffs out of Patrolman Hennessy's pocket in 1878 and walked away to escape arrest.

The other well-known type is the burglar who wears a collar. He is always referred to as a Raffles in real life. He is invariably a gentleman by daylight, breakfasting in a dress suit, and posing as a paperhanger, while after dark he plies his nefarious occupation of burglary. His mother is an extremely wealthy and respected resident of Ocean Grove, and when he is conducted to his cell he asks at once for a nail file and the Police Gazette. He always has a wife in every State in the Union and fiancées in all the Territories, and the newspapers print his matrimonial gallery out of their stock of cuts of the ladies who were cured by only one bottle after having been given up by five doctors, experiencing great relief after the first dose.

The burglar wore a blue sweater. He was neither a Raffles nor one of the chefs from Hell's Kitchen. The police would have been baffled had they attempted to classify him. They have not yet heard of the respectable, unassuming burglar who is neither above nor below his station.

This burglar of the third class began to prowl. He wore no masks, dark lanterns, or gumshoes. He carried a 38-calibre revolver in his pocket, and he chewed peppermint gum thoughtfully.

The furniture of the house was swathed in its summer dust protectors. The silver was far away in safe-deposit vaults. The burglar expected no remarkable "haul." His objective point was that dimly lighted room where the master of the house should be sleeping heavily after whatever solace he had sought to lighten the burden of his loneliness. A "touch" might be made there to the extent of legitimate, fair professional profits–loose money, a watch, a jeweled stickpin–nothing exorbitant or beyond reason. He had seen the window left open and had taken the chance.

The burglar softly opened the door of the lighted room. The gas was turned low. A man lay in the bed asleep. On the dresser lay many things in confusion–a crumpled roll of bills, a watch, keys, three poker chips, crushed cigars, a pink silk hair bow, and an unopened bottle of bromo-seltzer for a bulwark in the morning.

The burglar took three steps toward the dresser. The man in the bed suddenly uttered a squeaky groan and opened his eyes. His right hand slid under his pillow, but remained there.

"Lay still," said the burglar in conversational tone. Burglars of the third type do not hiss. The citizen in the bed looked at the round end of the burglar's pistol and lay still.

"Now hold up both your hands," commanded the burglar.

The citizen had a little, pointed, brown-and-gray beard, like that of a painless dentist. He looked solid, esteemed, irritable, and disgusted. He sat up in bed and raised his right hand above his head.

"Up with the other one," ordered the burglar. "You might be amphibious and shoot with your left. You can count two, can't you? Hurry up, now."

"Can't raise the other one," said the citizen, with a contortion of his lineaments.

"What's the matter with it?"

"Rheumatism in the shoulder."

"Inflammatory?"

"Was. The inflammation has gone down."

The burglar stood for a moment or two, holding his gun on the afflicted one. He glanced at the plunder on the dresser and then, with a half-embarrassed air, back at the man in the bed. Then he, too, made a sudden grimace.

"Don't stand there making faces," snapped the citizen, bad-humoredly. "If you've come to burgle why don't you do it? There's some stuff lying around."

"'Scuse me," said the burglar, with a grin; "but it just socked me one, too. It's good for you that rheumatism and me happens to be old pals. I got it in my left arm, too. Most anybody but me would have popped you when you wouldn't hoist that left claw of yours."

"How long have you had it?" inquired the citizen.

"Four years. I guess that ain't all. Once you've got it, it's you for a rheumatic life–that's my judgment."

"Ever try rattlesnake oil?" asked the citizen, interestedly.

"Gallons," said the burglar. "If all the snakes I've used the oil of was strung out in a row they'd reach eight times as far as Saturn, and the rattles could be heard at Valparaiso, Indiana, and back."

"Some use Chiselum's Pills," remarked the citizen.

"Fudge!" said the burglar. "Took 'em five months. No good. I had some relief the year I tried Finkelham's Extract, Balm of Gilead poultices and Potts's Pain Pulverizer; but I think it was the buckeye I carried in my pocket what done the trick."

"Is yours worse in the morning or at night?" asked the citizen.

"Night," said the burglar; "just when I'm busiest. Say, take down that arm of yours–I guess you won't–Say! did you ever try Blickerstaff's Blood Builder?"

"I never did. Does yours come in paroxysms or is it a steady pain?"

The burglar sat down on the foot of the bed and rested his gun on his crossed knee.

"It jumps," said he. "It strikes me when I ain't looking for it. I had to give up second-story work because I got stuck sometimes half-way up. Tell you what–I don't believe the bloomin' doctors know what is good for it."

"Same here. I've spent a thousand dollars without getting any relief. Yours swell any?"

"Of mornings. And when it's goin' to rain–great Christopher!"

"Me, too," said the citizen. "I can tell when a streak of humidity the size of a table-cloth starts from Florida on its way to New York. And if I pass a theatre where there's an 'East Lynne' matinee going on, the moisture starts my left arm jumping like a toothache."

"It's undiluted–hades!" said the burglar. "You're dead right," said the citizen.

The burglar looked down at his pistol and thrust it into his pocket with an awkward attempt at ease.

"Say, old man," he said, constrainedly, "ever try opodeldoc?"

"Slop!" said the citizen angrily. "Might as well rub on restaurant butter."

"Sure," concurred the burglar. "It's a salve suitable for little Minnie when the kitty scratches her finger. I'll tell you what! We're up against it. I only find one thing that eases her up. Hey? Little old sanitary, ameliorating, lest-we-forget Booze. Say–this job's off–'scuse me–get on your clothes and let's go out and have some. 'Scuse the liberty, but–ouch! There she goes again!"

"For a week," said the citizen. "I haven't been able to dress myself without help. I'm afraid Thomas is in bed, and–"

"Climb out," said the burglar, "I'll help you get into your duds."

The conventional returned as a tidal wave and flooded the citizen. He stroked his brown-and-gray beard.

"It's very unusual," he began.

"Here's your shirt," said the burglar, "fall out. I knew a man who said Omberry's Ointment fixed him in two weeks so he could use both hands in tying his four-in-hand."

As they were going out the door the citizen turned and started back.

"'Liked to forgot my money," he explained; "laid it on the dresser last night."

The burglar caught him by the right sleeve.

"Come on," he said bluffly. "I ask you. Leave it alone. I've got the price. Ever try witch hazel and oil of wintergreen?"

At Arms *with* Morpheus

never could quite understand how Tom Hopkins came to make that blunder, for he had been through a whole term at a medical college–before he inherited his aunt's fortune–and had been considered strong in therapeutics.

We had been making a call together that evening, and afterward Tom ran up to my rooms for a pipe and a chat before going on to his own luxurious apartments. I had stepped into the other room for a moment when I heard Tom sing out:

"Oh, Billy, I'm going to take about four grains of quinine, if you don't mind– I'm feeling all blue and shivery. Guess I'm taking cold."

"All right," I called back. "The bottle is on the second shelf. Take it in a spoonful of that elixir of eucalyptus. It knocks the bitter out."

After I came back we sat by the fire and got our briars going. In about eight minutes Tom sank back into a gentle collapse.

I went straight to the medicine cabinet and looked.

"You unmitigated hayseed!" I growled. "See what money will do for a man's brains!"

There stood the morphine bottle with the stopple out, just as Tom had left it.

I routed out another young M.D. who roomed on the floor above, and sent him for old Doctor Gales, two squares away. Tom Hopkins has too much money to be attended by rising young practitioners alone.

When Gales came we put Tom through as expensive a course of treatment as the resources of the profession permit. After the more drastic remedies we gave him citrate of caffeine in frequent doses and strong coffee, and walked him up and down the floor between two of us. Old Gales pinched him and slapped his face and worked hard for the big check he could see in the distance. The young M.D. from the next floor gave Tom a most hearty, rousing kick, and then apologized to me.

"Couldn't help it," he said. "I never kicked a millionaire before in my life. I may never have another opportunity."

"Now," said Doctor Gales, after a couple of hours, "he'll do. But keep him awake for another hour. You can do that by talking to him and shaking him up occasionally. When his pulse and respiration are normal then let him sleep. I'll leave him with you now."

I was left alone with Tom, whom we had laid on a couch. He lay very still, and his eyes were half closed. I began my work of keeping him awake.

"Well, old man," I said, "you've had a narrow squeak, but we've pulled you through. When you were attending lectures, Tom, didn't any of the professors ever casually remark that m-o-r-p-h-i-a never spells 'quinia,' especially in four-grain doses? But I won't pile it up on you until you get on your feet. But you ought to have been a druggist, Tom; you're splendidly qualified to fill prescriptions."

Tom looked at me with a faint and foolish smile.

"B'ly," he murmured, "I feel jus' like a hum'n bird flyin' around a jolly lot of most 'shpensive roses. Don' bozzer me. Goin' sleep now."

And he went to sleep in two seconds. I shook him by the shoulder.

"Now, Tom," I said, severely, "this won't do. The big doctor said you must stay awake for at least an hour. Open your eyes. You're not entirely safe yet, you know. Wake up."

Tom Hopkins weighs one hundred and ninety-eight. He gave me another somnolent grin, and fell into deeper slumber. I would have made him move about, but I might as well have tried to make Cleopatra's needle waltz around the room with me. Tom's breathing became stertorous, and that, in connection with morphia poisoning, means danger.

Then I began to think. I could not rouse his body; I must strive to excite his mind. "Make him angry," was an idea that suggested itself. "Good!" I thought; but how? There was not a joint in Tom's armor. Dear old fellow! He was good nature itself, and a gallant gentleman, fine and true and clean as sunlight. He came from somewhere down South, where they still have ideals and a code. New York had charmed, but had not spoiled, him. He had that old-fashioned chivalrous reverence for women, that–Eureka!–there was my idea! I worked the thing up for a minute or two in my imagination. I chuckled to myself at the thought of springing a thing like that on old Tom Hopkins. Then I took him by the shoulder and shook him till his ears flopped. He opened his eyes lazily. I assumed an expression of scorn and contempt, and pointed my finger within two inches of his nose.

"Listen to me, Hopkins," I said, in cutting and distinct tones, "you and I have been good friends, but I want you to understand that in the future my doors are closed against any man who acts as much like a scoundrel as you have."

Tom looked the least bit interested.

"What's the matter, Billy?" he muttered, composedly. "Don't your clothes fit you?"

"If I were in your place," I went on, "which, thank God, I am not, I think I would be afraid to close my eyes. How about that girl you left waiting for you down among those lonesome Southern pines–the girl that you've forgotten since you came into your confounded money? Oh, I know what I'm talking about. While you were a poor medical student she was good enough for you. But now, since you are a millionaire, it's different. I wonder what she thinks of the performances of that peculiar class of people which she has been taught to worship–the Southern gentlemen? I'm sorry, Hopkins, that I was forced to speak about these matters, but you've covered it up so well and played your part so nicely that I would have sworn you were above such unmanly tricks."

Poor Tom. I could scarcely keep from laughing outright to see him struggling against the effects of the opiate. He was distinctly angry, and I didn't blame him. Tom had a Southern temper. His eyes were open now, and they showed a gleam or two of fire. But the drug still clouded his mind and bound his tongue.

"C-c-confound you," he stammered, "I'll s-smash you."

He tried to rise from the couch. With all his size he was very weak now. I thrust him back with one arm. He lay there glaring like a lion in a trap.

"That will hold you for a while, you old loony," I said to myself. I got up and lit my pipe, for I was needing a smoke. I walked around a bit, congratulating myself on my brilliant idea.

I heard a snore. I looked around. Tom was asleep again. I walked over and punched him on the jaw. He looked at me as pleasant and ungrudging as an idiot. I chewed my pipe and gave it to him hard.

"I want you to recover yourself and get out of my rooms as soon as you can," I said, insultingly. "I've told you what I think of you. If you have any honor or honesty left you will think twice before you attempt again to associate with gentlemen. She's a poor girl, isn't she?" I sneered. "Somewhat too plain and unfashionable for us since we got our money. Be ashamed to walk on Fifth Avenue with her, wouldn't you? Hopkins, you're forty-seven times worse than a cad. Who cares for your money? I don't. I'll bet that girl don't. Perhaps if you didn't have it you'd be more of a man. As it is you've made a cur of yourself, and"–I thought that quite dramatic–"perhaps broken a faithful heart." (Old Tom Hopkins breaking a faithful heart!) "Let me be rid of you as soon as possible."

I turned my back on Tom, and winked at myself in a mirror. I heard him moving, and I turned again quickly. I didn't want a hundred and ninety-eight pounds falling on me from the rear. But Tom had only turned partly over, and laid one arm across his face. He spoke a few words rather more distinctly than before.

"I couldn't have–talked this way–to you, Billy, even if I'd heard people–lyin' 'bout you. But jus' soon's I can s-stand up–I'll break your neck–don' f'get it."

I did feel a little ashamed then. But it was to save Tom. In the morning, when I explained it, we would have a good laugh over it together.

In about twenty minutes Tom dropped into a sound, easy slumber. I felt his pulse, listened to his respiration, and let him sleep. Everything was normal, and Tom was safe. I went into the other room and tumbled into bed.

I found Tom up and dressed when I awoke the next morning. He was entirely himself again with the exception of shaky nerves and a tongue like a white-oak chip.

"What an idiot I was," he said, thoughtfully. "I remember thinking that quinine bottle looked queer while I was taking the dose. Have much trouble in bringing me 'round?"

I told him no. His memory seemed bad about the entire affair. I concluded that he had no recollection of my efforts to keep him awake, and decided not to enlighten him. Some other time, I thought, when he was feeling better, we would have some fun over it.

When Tom was ready to go he stopped, with the door open, and shook my hand.

"Much obliged, old fellow," he said, quietly, "for taking so much trouble with me–and for what you said. I'm going down now to telegraph to the little girl."

A Ghost *of a* Chance

ctually, a hod!" repeated Mrs. Kinsolving, pathetically.

Mrs. Bellamy Bellmore arched a sympathetic eyebrow. Thus, she expressed condolence and a generous amount of apparent surprise.

"Fancy her telling everywhere," recapitulated Mrs. Kinsolving, "that she saw a ghost in the apartment she occupied here–our choicest guest-room–a ghost, carrying a hod on its shoulder–the ghost of an old man in overalls, smoking a pipe and carrying a hod! The very absurdity of the thing shows her malicious intent. There never was a Kinsolving that carried a hod. Everyone knows that Mr. Kinsolving's father accumulated his money by large building contracts, but he never worked a day with his own hands. He had this house built from his own plans; but– oh, a hod! Why need she have been so cruel and malicious?"

"It is really too bad," murmured Mrs. Bellmore, with an approving glance of her fine eyes about the vast chamber done in lilac and old gold. "And it was in this room she saw it! Oh, no, I'm not afraid of ghosts. Don't have the least fear on my account. I'm glad you put me in here. I think family ghosts so interesting! But, really, the story does sound a little inconsistent. I should have expected something better from Mrs. Fischer-Suympkins. Don't they carry bricks in hods? Why should a ghost bring bricks into a villa built of marble and stone? I'm so sorry, but it makes me think that age is beginning to tell upon Mrs. Fischer-Suympkins."

"This house," continued Mrs. Kinsolving, "was built upon the site of an old one used by the family during the Revolution. There wouldn't be anything strange in its having a ghost. And there was a Captain Kinsolving who fought in General Greene's army, though we've never been able to secure any papers to vouch for it. If there is to be a family ghost, why couldn't it have been his, instead of a bricklayer's?"

"The ghost of a Revolutionary ancestor wouldn't be a bad idea," agreed Mrs. Bellmore; "but you know how arbitrary and inconsiderate ghosts can be. Maybe, like love, they are 'engendered in the eye.' One advantage of those who see ghosts is that their stories can't be disproved. By a spiteful eye, a Revolutionary knapsack might easily be construed to be a hod. Dear Mrs. Kinsolving, think no more of it. I am sure it was a knapsack."

"But she told everybody!" mourned Mrs. Kinsolving, inconsolable. "She insisted upon the details. There is the pipe. And how are you going to get out of the overalls?"

"Shan't get into them," said Mrs. Bellmore, with a prettily suppressed yawn; "too stiff and wrinkly. Is that you, Felice? Prepare my bath, please. Do you dine at seven at Clifftop, Mrs. Kinsolving? So kind of you to run in for a chat before dinner! I love those little touches of informality with a guest. They give such a home flavor to a visit. So sorry; I must be dressing. I am so indolent I always postpone it until the last moment."

Mrs. Fischer-Suympkins had been the first large plum that the Kinsolvings had drawn from the social pie. For a long time, the pie itself had been out of reach on a top shelf. But the purse and the pursuit had at last lowered it. Mrs. Fischer-Suympkins was the heliograph of the smart society parading corps. The glitter of her wit and actions passed along the line, transmitting whatever was latest and most daring in the game of peep-show. Formerly, her fame and leadership had been secure enough not to need the support of such artifices as handing around live frogs for favors at a cotillion. But, now, these things were necessary to the holding of her throne. Besides, middle age had come to preside, incongruous, at her capers. The sensational papers had cut her space from a page to two columns. Her wit developed a sting; her manners became rougher and more inconsiderate, as if she felt the royal necessity of establishing her autocracy by scorning the conventionalities that bound lesser potentates.

To some pressure at the command of the Kinsolvings, she had yielded so far as to honor their house by her presence, for an evening and night. She had her revenge upon her hostess by relating, with grim enjoyment and sarcastic humor, her story of the vision carrying the hod. To that lady, in raptures at having penetrated thus far toward the coveted inner circle, the result came as a crushing disappointment. Everybody either sympathized or laughed, and there was little to choose between the two modes of expression.

But, later on, Mrs. Kinsolving's hopes and spirits were revived by the capture of a second and greater prize.

Mrs. Bellamy Bellmore had accepted an invitation to visit at Clifftop, and would remain for three days. Mrs. Bellmore was one of the younger matrons, whose beauty, descent, and wealth gave her a reserved seat in the holy of holies that required no strenuous bolstering. She was generous enough thus to give Mrs. Kinsolving the accolade that was so poignantly desired; and, at the same time, she thought how much it would please Terence. Perhaps it would end by solving him.

Terence was Mrs. Kinsolving's son, aged twenty-nine, quite good-looking enough, and with two or three attractive and mysterious traits. For one, he was very devoted to his mother, and that was sufficiently odd to deserve notice. For others, he talked so little that it was irritating, and he seemed either very shy or very deep. Terence interested Mrs. Bellmore, because she was not sure which it was. She intended to study him a little longer, unless she forgot the matter. If he was only shy, she would abandon him, for shyness is a bore. If he was deep, she would also abandon him, for depth is precarious.

On the afternoon of the third day of her visit, Terence hunted up Mrs. Bellmore, and found her in a nook actually looking at an album.

"It's so good of you," said he, "to come down here and retrieve the day for us. I suppose you have heard that Mrs. Fischer-Suympkins scuttled the ship before she left. She knocked a whole plank out of the bottom with a hod. My mother is grieving herself ill about it. Can't you manage to see a ghost for us while you are here, Mrs. Bellmore—a bang-up, swell ghost, with a coronet on his head and a cheque book under his arm?"

"That was a naughty old lady, Terence," said Mrs. Bellmore, "to tell such stories. Perhaps you gave her too much supper. Your mother doesn't really take it seriously, does she?"

"I think she does," answered Terence. "One would think every brick in the hod had dropped on her. It's a good mammy, and I don't like to see her worried. It's to be hoped that the ghost belongs to the hod-carriers' union, and will go out on a strike. If he doesn't, there will be no peace in this family."

"I'm sleeping in the ghost-chamber," said Mrs. Bellmore, pensively. "But it's so nice I wouldn't change it, even if I were afraid, which I'm not. It wouldn't do for me to submit a counter story of a desirable, aristocratic shade, would it? I would do so, with pleasure, but it seems to me it would be too obviously an antidote for the other narrative to be effective."

"True," said Terence, running two fingers thoughtfully into his crisp, brown hair; "that would never do. How would it work to see the same ghost again, minus the overalls, and have gold bricks in the hod? That would elevate the specter from degrading toil to a financial plane. Don't you think that would be respectable enough?"

"There was an ancestor who fought against the Britishers, wasn't there? Your mother said something to that effect."

"I believe so; one of those old chaps in raglan vests and golf trousers. I don't care a continental for a Continental, myself. But the mother has set her heart on pomp and heraldry and pyrotechnics, and I want her to be happy."

"You are a good boy, Terence," said Mrs. Bellmore, sweeping her silks close to one side of her, "not to beat your mother. Sit here by me, and let's look at the album, just as people used to do twenty years ago. Now, tell me about every one of them. Who is this tall, dignified gentleman leaning against the horizon, with one arm on the Corinthian column?"

"That old chap with the big feet?" inquired Terence, craning his neck. "That's great-uncle O'Brannigan. He used to keep a *rathskeller* on the Bowery."

"I asked you to sit down, Terence. If you are not going to amuse, or obey, me, I shall report in the morning that I saw a ghost wearing an apron and carrying schooners of beer. Now, that is better. To be shy, at your age, Terence, is a thing that you should blush to acknowledge."

At breakfast on the last morning of her visit, Mrs. Bellmore startled and entranced every one present by announcing positively that she had seen the ghost.

"Did it have a–a–a–?" Mrs. Kinsolving, in her suspense and agitation, could not bring out the word.

"No, indeed–far from it."

There was a chorus of questions from others at the table. "Weren't you frightened?" "What did it do?" "How did it look?" "How was it dressed?" "Did it say anything?" "Didn't you scream?"

"I'll try to answer everything at once," said Mrs. Bellmore, heroically, "although I'm frightfully hungry. Something awakened me–I'm not sure whether it was a noise or a touch–and there stood the phantom. I never burn a light at night, so the room was quite dark, but I saw it plainly. I wasn't dreaming. It was a tall man, all misty white from head to foot. It wore the full dress of the old Colonial days–powdered hair, baggy coat skirts, lace ruffles, and a sword. It looked intangible and luminous in the dark, and moved without a sound. Yes, I was a little frightened at first–or startled, I should say. It was the first ghost I had ever seen. No, it didn't say anything. I didn't scream. I raised up on my elbow, and then it glided silently away, and disappeared when it reached the door."

Mrs. Kinsolving was in the seventh heaven. "The description is that of Captain Kinsolving, of General Greene's army, one of our ancestors," she said, in a voice that trembled with pride and relief. "I really think I must apologize for our ghostly relative, Mrs. Bellmore. I am afraid he must have badly disturbed your rest."

Terence sent a smile of pleased congratulation toward his mother. Attainment was Mrs. Kinsolving's, at last, and he loved to see her happy.

"I suppose I ought to be ashamed to confess," said Mrs. Bellmore, who was now enjoying her breakfast, "that I wasn't very much disturbed. I presume it would have been the customary thing to scream and faint, and have all of you running about in picturesque costumes. But, after the first alarm was over, I really couldn't work myself up to a panic. The ghost retired from the stage quietly and peacefully, after doing its little turn, and I went to sleep again."

Nearly all listened, politely accepted Mrs. Bellmore s story as a made-up affair, charitably offered as an offset to the unkind vision seen by Mrs. Fischer-Suympkins. But one or two present perceived that her assertions bore the genuine stamp of her own convictions. Truth and candor seemed to attend upon every word. Even a scoffer at ghosts–if he were very observant– would have been forced to admit that she had, at least in a very vivid dream, been honestly aware of the weird visitor.'

Soon Mrs. Bellmore's maid was packing. In two hours the auto would come to convey her to the station. As Terence was strolling upon the east piazza, Mrs. Bellmore came up to him, with a confidential sparkle in her eye.

"I didn't wish to tell the others all of it," she said, "but I will tell you. In a way, I think you should be held responsible. Can you guess in what manner that ghost awakened me last night?"

"Rattled chains," suggested Terence, after some thought, "or groaned? They usually do one or the other."

"Do you happen to know," continued Mrs. Bellmore, with sudden irrelevancy, "if I resemble any one of the female relatives of your restless ancestor, Captain Kinsolving?"

"Don't think so," said Terence, with an extremely puzzled air. "Never heard of any of them being noted beauties."

"Then, why," said Mrs. Bellmore, looking the young man gravely in the eye, "should that ghost have kissed me, as I'm sure it did?"

"Heavens!" exclaimed Terence, in wide-eyed amazement; "you don't mean that, Mrs. Bellmore! Did he actually kiss you?"

"I said it," corrected Mrs. Bellmore. "I hope the impersonal pronoun is correctly used."

"But why did you say I was responsible?"

"Because you are the only living male relative of the ghost."

"I see. 'Unto the third and fourth generation.' But, seriously, did he–did it–how do you–?"

"Know? How does anyone know? I was asleep, and that is what awakened me, I'm almost certain."

"Almost?"

"Well, I awoke just as–oh, can't you understand what I mean? When anything arouses you suddenly, you are not positive whether you dreamed, or– and yet you know that– Dear me, Terence, must I dissect the most elementary sensations in order to accommodate your extremely practical intelligence?"

"But, about kissing ghosts, you know," said Terence, humbly, "I require the most primary instruction. I never kissed a ghost. Is it–is it–?"

"The sensation," said Mrs. Bellmore, with deliberate, but slightly smiling, emphasis, "since you are seeking instruction, is a mingling of the material and the spiritual."

"Of course," said Terence, suddenly growing serious, "it was a dream or some kind of an hallucination. Nobody believes in spirits, these days. If you told the tale out of kindness of heart, Mrs. Bellmore, I can't express how grateful I am to you. It has made my mother supremely happy. That Revolutionary ancestor was a stunning idea."

Mrs. Bellmore sighed. "The usual fate of ghost-seers is mine," she said, resignedly. "My privileged encounter with a spirit is attributed to lobster salad or mendacity. Well, I have, at least, one memory left from the wreck–a kiss from the unseen world. Was Captain Kinsolving a very brave man, do you know, Terence?"

"He was licked at Yorktown, I believe," said Terence, reflecting. "They say he skedaddled with his company, after the first battle there."

"I thought he must have been timid," said Mrs. Bellmore, absently. "He might have had another."

"Another battle?" asked Terence, dully.

"What else could I mean? I must go and get ready now; the auto will be here in an hour. I've enjoyed Clifftop immensely. Such a lovely morning, isn't it, Terence?"

On her way to the station, Mrs. Bellmore took from her bag a silk handkerchief, and looked at it with a little peculiar smile. Then she tied it in several very hard knots, and threw it, at a convenient moment, over the edge of the cliff along which the road ran.

In his room, Terence was giving some directions to his man, Brooks. "Have this stuff done up in a parcel," he said, "and ship it to the address on that card."

The card was that of a New York costumer. The "stuff" was a gentleman's costume of the days of '76, made of white satin, with silver buckles, white silk stockings, and white kid shoes. A powdered wig and a sword completed the dress.

"And look about, Brooks," added Terence, a little anxiously, "for a silk handkerchief with my initials in one corner. I must have dropped it somewhere."

It was a month later when Mrs. Bellmore and one or two others of the smart crowd were making up a list of names for a coaching trip through the Catskills. Mrs. Bellmore looked over the list for a final censoring. The name of Terence Kinsolving was there. Mrs. Bellmore ran her prohibitive pencil lightly through the name.

"Too shy!" she murmured, sweetly, in explanation.

Jimmy Hayes *and* Muriel

I

upper was over, and there had fallen upon the camp the silence that accompanies the rolling of cornhusk cigarettes. The water hole shone from the dark earth like a patch of fallen sky. Coyotes yelped. Dull thumps indicated the rocking-horse movements of the hobbled ponies as they moved to fresh grass. A half-troop of the Frontier Battalion of Texas Rangers were distributed about the fire.

A well-known sound–the fluttering and scraping of chaparral against wooden stirrups–came from the thick brush above the camp. The rangers listened cautiously. They heard a loud and cheerful voice call out reassuringly:

"Brace up, Muriel, old girl, we're 'most there now! Been a long ride for ye, ain't it, ye old antediluvian handful of animated carpet-tacks? Hey, now, quit a tryin' to kiss me! Don't hold on to my neck so tight–this here paint hoss ain't any too shore-footed, let me tell ye. He's liable to dump us both off if we don't watch out."

Two minutes of waiting brought a tired "paint" pony single-footing into camp. A gangling youth of twenty lolled in the saddle. Of the "Muriel" whom he had been addressing, nothing was to be seen.

"Hi, fellows!" shouted the rider cheerfully. "This here's a letter fer Lieutenant Manning."

He dismounted, unsaddled, dropped the coils of his stake-rope, and got his hobbles from the saddle-horn. While Lieutenant Manning, in command, was reading the letter, the newcomer, rubbed solicitously at some dried mud in the loops of the hobbles, showing a consideration for the forelegs of his mount.

"Boys," said the lieutenant, waving his hand to the rangers, "this is Mr. James Hayes. He's a new member of the company. Captain McLean sends him down from El Paso. The boys will see that you have some supper, Hayes, as soon as you get your pony hobbled."

The recruit was received cordially by the rangers. Still, they observed him shrewdly and with suspended judgment. Picking a comrade on the border is done with ten times the care and discretion with which a girl chooses a sweetheart. On your "side-kicker's" nerve, loyalty, aim, and coolness your own life may depend many times.

After a hearty supper Hayes joined the smokers about the fire. His appearance did not settle all the questions in the minds of his brother rangers. They saw simply a loose, lank youth with tow-colored, sunburned hair and a berry-brown, ingenuous face that wore a quizzical, good-natured smile.

"Fellows," said the new ranger, "I'm goin' to interduce to you a lady friend of mine. Ain't ever heard anybody call her a beauty, but you'll all admit she's got some fine points about her. Come along, Muriel!"

He held open the front of his blue flannel shirt. Out of it crawled a horned frog. A bright red ribbon was tied jauntily around its spiky neck. It crawled to its owner's knee and sat there, motionless.

"This here Muriel," said Hayes, with an oratorical wave of his hand, "has got qualities. She never talks back, she always stays at home, and she's satisfied with one red dress for every day and Sunday, too."

"Look at that blame insect!" said one of the rangers with a grin. "I've seen plenty of them horny frogs, but I never knew anybody to have one for a side-partner. Does the blame thing know you from anybody else?"

"Take it over there and see," said Hayes.

The stumpy little lizard known as the horned frog is harmless. He has the hideousness of the prehistoric monsters whose reduced descendant he is, but he is gentler than the dove.

The ranger took Muriel from Hayes's knee and went back to his seat on a roll of blankets. The captive twisted and clawed and struggled vigorously in his hand. After holding it for a moment or two, the ranger set it upon the ground. Awkwardly, but swiftly the frog worked its four oddly moving legs until it stopped close by Hayes's foot.

"Well, dang my hide!" said the other ranger. "The little cuss knows you. Never thought them insects had that much sense!"

II

Jimmy Hayes became a favorite in the ranger camp. He had an endless store of good-nature, and a mild, perennial quality of humor that is well adapted to camp life. He was never without his horned frog. In the bosom of his shirt during rides, on his knee or shoulder in camp, under his blankets at night, the ugly little beast never left him.

Jimmy was a humorist of a type that prevails in the rural South and West. Unskilled in originating methods of amusing or in witty conceptions, he had hit upon a comical idea and clung to it reverently. It had seemed to Jimmy a very funny thing to have about his person, with which to amuse his friends, a tame horned frog with a red ribbon around its neck. As it was a happy idea, why not perpetuate it?

The sentiments existing between Jimmy and the frog cannot be exactly determined. The capability of the horned frog for lasting affection is a subject upon which we have had no symposiums. It is easier to guess Jimmy's feelings. Muriel was his chef d'oeuvre of wit, and as such he cherished her. He caught flies for her, and shielded her from sudden northers. Yet his care was half selfish, and when the time came, she repaid him a thousand-fold. Other Muriels have thus overbalanced the light attentions of other Jimmies.

Not at once did Jimmy Hayes attain full brotherhood with his comrades. They loved him for his simplicity and drollness, but there hung above him a great sword of suspended judgment. To make merry in camp is not all of a ranger's life. There are horse-thieves to trail, desperate criminals to run down, bravos to battle with, bandits to rout out of the chaparral, peace and order to be compelled at the muzzle of a six-shooter. Jimmy had been "'most generally a cowpuncher," he said; he was inexperienced in ranger methods of warfare. Therefore, the rangers speculated apart and solemnly as to how he would stand fire. For, let it be known, the honor and pride of each ranger company is the individual bravery of its members.

For two months the border was quiet. The rangers lolled, listless, in camp. And then–bringing joy to the rusting guardians of the frontier–Sebastiano Saldar, an eminent Mexican desperado and cattle-thief, crossed the Rio Grande with his gang and began to lay waste the Texas side. There were indications that Jimmy Hayes would soon have the opportunity to show his mettle. The rangers patrolled with alacrity, but Saldar's men were mounted like Lochinvar, and were hard to catch.

One evening, about sundown, the rangers halted for supper after a long ride. Their horses stood panting, with their saddles on. The men were frying bacon and boiling coffee. Suddenly, out of the brush, Sebastiano Saldar and his gang dashed upon them with blazing six-shooters and high-voiced yells. It was a neat surprise. The rangers swore in annoyed tones, and got their Winchesters busy; but the attack was only a spectacular dash of the purest Mexican type. After the florid demonstration the raiders galloped away, yelling, down the river. The rangers mounted and pursued; but in less than two miles the fagged ponies labored so that Lieutenant Manning gave the word to abandon the chase and return to the camp.

Then it was discovered that Jimmy Hayes was missing. Someone remembered having seen him run for his pony when the attack began, but no one had set eyes on him since. Morning came, but no Jimmy. They searched the country around, on the theory that he had been killed or wounded, but without success. Then they followed after Saldar's gang, but it seemed to have disappeared. Manning concluded that the wily Mexican had recrossed the river after his theatric farewell. And, indeed, no further depredations from him were reported.

This gave the rangers time to nurse a soreness they had. As has been said, the pride and honor of the company is the individual bravery of its members. And now they believed that Jimmy Hayes had turned coward at the whiz of Mexican bullets. There was no other deduction. Buck Davis pointed out that not a shot was fired by Saldar's gang after Jimmy was seen running for his horse. There was no way for him to have been shot. No, he had fled from his first fight, and afterward he would not return, aware that the scorn of his comrades would be a worse thing to face than the muzzles of many rifles.

So Manning's detachment of McLean's company, Frontier Battalion, was gloomy. It was the first blot on its escutcheon. Never before in the history of the service had a ranger shown the white feather. All of them had liked Jimmy Hayes, and that made it worse.

Days, weeks, and months went by, and still that little cloud of unforgotten cowardice hung above the camp.

III

Nearly a year afterward–after many camping grounds and many hundreds of miles guarded and defended–Lieutenant Manning, with almost the same detachment of men, was sent to a point only a few miles below their old camp on the river to look after some smuggling there. One afternoon, while they were riding through a dense mesquite flat, they came upon a patch of open hog-wallow prairie. There they rode upon the scene of an unwritten tragedy.

In a big hog-wallow lay the skeletons of three Mexicans. Their clothing alone served to identify them. The largest of the figures had once been Sebastiano Saldar. His great, costly sombrero, heavy with gold ornamentation– a hat famous all along the Rio Grande–lay there pierced by three bullets. Along the ridge of the hog-wallow rested the rusting Winchesters of the Mexicans–all pointing in the same direction.

The rangers rode in that direction for fifty yards. There, in a little depression of the ground, with his rifle still bearing upon the three, lay another skeleton. It had been a battle of extermination. There was nothing to identify the solitary defender. His clothing–such as the elements had left distinguishable–seemed to be of the kind that any ranchman or cowboy might have worn.

"Some cow-puncher," said Manning, "that they caught out alone. Good boy! He put up a dandy scrap before they got him. So that's why we didn't hear from Don Sebastiano anymore!"

And then, from beneath the weather-beaten rags of the dead man, there wriggled out a horned frog with a faded red ribbon around its neck, and sat upon the shoulder of its long quiet master. Mutely it told the story of the untried youth and the swift "paint" pony–how they had outstripped all their comrades that day in the pursuit of the Mexican raiders, and how the boy had gone down upholding the honor of the company.

The ranger troop herded close, and a simultaneous wild yell arose from their lips. The outburst was at once a dirge, an apology, an epitaph, and a paean of triumph. A strange requiem, you may say, over the body of a fallen, comrade; but if Jimmy Hayes could have heard it he would have understood.

The Door *of* Unrest

sat an hour by sun, in the editor's room of the Montopolis Weekly Bugle. I was the editor.

The saffron rays of the declining sunlight filtered through the cornstalks in Micajah Widdup's garden-patch, and cast an amber glory upon my paste-pot. I sat at the editorial desk in my non-rotary revolving chair, and prepared my editorial against the oligarchies. The room, with its one window, was already a prey to the twilight. One by one, with my trenchant sentences, I lopped off the heads of the political hydra, while I listened, full of kindly peace, to the home-coming cow-bells and wondered what Mrs. Flanagan was going to have for supper.

Then in from the dusky, quiet street there drifted and perched himself upon a corner of my desk old Father Time's younger brother. His face was beardless and as gnarled as an English walnut. I never saw clothes such as he wore. They would have reduced Joseph's coat to a monochrome. But the colors were not the dyer's. Stains and patches and the work of sun and rust were responsible for the diversity. On his coarse shoes was the dust, conceivably, of a thousand leagues. I can describe him no further, except to say that he was little and weird and old–old I began to estimate in centuries when I saw him. Yes, and I remember that there was an odor, a faint odor like aloes, or possibly like myrrh or leather; and I thought of museums.

And then I reached for a pad and pencil, for business is business, and visits of the oldest inhabitants are sacred and honorable, requiring to be chronicled.

"I am glad to see you, sir," I said. "I would offer you a chair, but–you see, sir," I went on, "I have lived in Montopolis only three weeks, and I have not met many of our citizens." I turned a doubtful eye upon his dust-stained shoes, and concluded with a newspaper phrase, "I suppose that you reside in our midst?"

My visitor fumbled in his raiment, drew forth a soiled card, and handed it to me. Upon it was written, in plain but unsteadily formed characters, the name "Michob Ader."

"I am glad you called, Mr. Ader," I said. "As one of our older citizens, you must view with pride the recent growth and enterprise of Montopolis. Among other improvements, I think I can promise that the town will now be provided with a live, enterprising newspa–"

"Do ye know the name on that card?" asked my caller, interrupting me.

"It is not a familiar one to me," I said.

Again he visited the depths of his ancient vestments. This time he brought out a torn leaf of some book or journal, brown and flimsy with age. The heading of the page was the Turkish Spy in old-style type; the printing upon it was this:

"There is a man come to Paris in this year 1643 who pretends to have lived these sixteen hundred years. He says of himself that he was a shoemaker in Jerusalem at the time of the Crucifixion; that his name is Michob Ader; and that when Jesus, the Christian Messias, was condemned by Pontius Pilate, the Roman president, he paused to rest while bearing his cross to the place of crucifixion before the door of

Michob Ader. The shoemaker struck Jesus with his fist, saying: 'Go; why tarriest thou?' The Messias answered him: 'I indeed am going; but thou shalt tarry until I come'; thereby condemning him to live until the Day of Judgment. He lives forever, but at the end of every hundred years he falls into a fit or trance, on recovering from which he finds himself in the same state of youth in which he was when Jesus suffered, being thenabout thirty years of age.

"Such is the story of the Wandering Jew, as told by Michob Ader, who relates–" Here the printing ended.

I must have muttered aloud something to myself about the Wandering Jew, for the old man spake up, bitterly and loudly.

"'Tis a lie," said he, "like nine tenths of what ye call history. 'Tis a Gentile I am, and no Jew. I am after footing it out of Jerusalem, my son; but if that makes me a Jew, then everything that comes out of a bottle is babies' milk. Ye have my name on the card ye hold; and ye have read the bit of paper they call the Turkish Spy that printed the news when I stepped into their office on the 12th day of June, in the year 1643, just as I have called upon ye today."

I laid down my pencil and pad. Clearly it would not do. Here was an item for the local column of the Bugle that–but it would not do. Still, fragments of the impossible "personal" began to flit through my conventionalized brain. "Uncle Michob is as spry on his legs as a young chap of only a thousand or so." "Our venerable caller relates with pride that George Wash–no, Ptolemy the Great–once dandled him on his knee at his father's house." "Uncle Michob says that our wet spring was nothing in comparison with the dampness that ruined the crops around Mount Ararat when he was a boy–" But no, no–it would not do.

I was trying to think of some conversational subject with which to interest my visitor, and was hesitating between walking matches and the Pliocene age, when the old man suddenly began to weep poignantly and distressfully.

"Cheer up, Mr. Ader," I said, a little awkwardly; "this matter may blow over in a few hundred years more. There has already been a decided reaction in favour of Judas Iscariot and Colonel Burr and the celebrated violinist, Signor Nero. This is the age of whitewash. You must not allow yourself to become down-hearted."

Unknowingly, I had struck a chord. The old man blinked belligerently through his senile tears.

"'Tis time," he said, "that the liars be doin' justice to somebody. Yer historians are no more than a pack of old women gabblin' at a wake. A finer man than the Imperor Nero niver wore sandals. Man, I was at the burnin' of Rome. I knowed the Imperor well, for in them days I was a well-known character. In thim days they had rayspect for a man that lived forever.

"But 'twas of the Imperor Nero I was goin' to tell ye. I struck into Rome, up the Appian Way, on the night of July the 16th, the year 64. I had just stepped down by way of Siberia and Afghanistan; and one foot of me had a frost-bite, and the other a blister burned by the sand of the desert; and I was feelin' a bit blue from doin' patrol duty from the North Pole down to the Last Chance corner in Patagonia, and bein' miscalled a Jew in the bargain. Well, I'm tellin' ye I was passin' the Circus Maximus, and it was dark as pitch over the way, and then I heard somebody sing out, 'Is that you, Michob?'

"Over ag'inst the wall, hid out amongst a pile of barrels and old dry-goods boxes, was the Imperor Nero wid his togy wrapped around his toes, smokin' a long, black segar.

"'Have one, Michob?' says he.

"'None of the weeds for me,' says I–'nayther pipe nor segar. What's the use,' says I, 'of smokin' when ye've not got the ghost of a chance of killin' yeself by doin' it?'

"'True for ye, Michob Ader, my perpetual Jew,' says the Imperor; 'ye're not always wandering. Sure, 'tis danger gives the spice of our pleasures–next to their bein' forbidden.'

"'And for what,' says I, 'do ye smoke be night in dark places widout even a cinturion in plain clothes to attend ye?'

"'Have ye ever heard, Michob,' says the Imperor, 'of predestinarianism?'

"'I've had the cousin of it,' says I. 'I've been on the trot with pedestrianism for many a year, and more to come, as ye well know.'

"'The longer word,' says me friend Nero, 'is the tachin' of this new sect of people they call the Christians. 'Tis them that's raysponsible for me smokin' be night in holes and corners of the dark.'

"And then I sets down and takes off a shoe and rubs me foot that is frosted, and the Imperor tells me about it. It seems that since I passed that way before, the Imperor had mandamused the Impress wid a divorce suit, and Misses Poppaea, a cilibrated lady, was ingaged, widout riferences, as housekeeper at the palace. 'All in one day,' says the Imperor, 'she puts up new lace windy-curtains in the palace and joins the anti-tobacco society, and whin I feels the need of a smoke I must be after sneakin' out to these piles of lumber in the dark.' So there in the dark me and the Imperor sat, and I told him of me travels. And when they say the Imperor was an incindiary, they lie. 'Twas that night the fire started that burnt the city. 'Tis my opinion that it began from a stump of segar that he threw down among the boxes. And 'tis a lie that he fiddled. He did all he could for six days to stop it, sir."

And now I detected a new flavor to Mr. Michob Ader. It had not been myrrh or balm or hyssop that I had smelled. The emanation was the odor of bad whiskey–and, worse still, of low comedy–the sort that small humorists manufacture by clothing the grave and reverend things of legend and history in the vulgar, topical frippery that passes for a certain kind of wit. Michob Ader as an impostor, claiming nineteen hundred years, and playing his part with the decency of respectable lunacy, I could endure; but as a tedious wag, cheapening his egregious story with songbook levity, his importance as an entertainer grew less.

And then, as if he suspected my thoughts, he suddenly shifted his key.

"You'll excuse me, sir," he whined, "but sometimes I get a little mixed in my head. I am a very old man; and it is hard to remember everything."

I knew that he was right, and that I should not try to reconcile him with Roman history; so I asked for news concerning other ancients with whom he had walked familiar.

Above my desk hung an engraving of Raphael's cherubs. You could yet make out their forms, though the dust blurred their outlines strangely.

"Ye calls them 'cher-rubs'," cackled the old man. "Babes, ye fancy they are, with wings. And there's one wid legs and a bow and arrow that ye call Cupid–I know where they was found. The great-great-great-grandfather of thim all was a billy-goat. Bein' an editor, sir, do ye happen to know where Solomon s Temple stood?"

I fancied that it was in–in Persia? Well, I did not know.

"'Tis not in history nor in the Bible where it was. But I saw it, meself. The first pictures of cher-rubs and cupids was sculptured upon thim walls and pillars. Two of the biggest, sir, stood in the adytum to form the baldachin over the Ark. But the wings of thim sculptures was intindid for horns. And the faces was the faces of goats. Ten thousand goats there was in and about the temple. And your cher-rubs was billy-goats in the days of King Solomon, but the painters misconstrued the horns into wings.

"And I knew Tamerlane, the lame Timour, sir, very well. I saw him at Keghut and at Zaranj. He was a little man no larger than yerself, with hair the colour of an amber pipe stem. They buried him at Samarkand. I was at the wake, sir. Oh, he was a fine-built man in his coffin, six feet long, with black whiskers to his face. And I see 'em throw turnips at the Imperor Vispacian in Africa. All over the world I have tramped, sir, without the body of me findin' any rest. 'Twas so commanded. I saw Jerusalem destroyed, and Pompeii go up in the fireworks; and I was at the coronation of Charlemagne and the lynchin' of Joan of Arc. And everywhere I go there comes storms and revolutions and plagues and fires. 'Twas so commanded. Ye have heard of the Wandering Jew. 'Tis all so, except that divil a bit am I a Jew. But history lies, as I have told ye. Are ye quite sure, sir, that ye haven't a drop of whiskey convenient? Ye well know that I have many miles of walking before me."

"I have none," said I, "and, if you please, I am about to leave for my supper."

I pushed my chair back creakingly. This ancient landlubber was becoming as great an affliction as any cross-bowed mariner. He shook a musty effluvium from his piebald clothes, overturned my inkstand, and went on with his insufferable nonsense.

"I wouldn't mind it so much," he complained, "if it wasn't for the work I must do on Good Fridays. Ye know about Pontius Pilate, sir, of course. His body, whin he killed himself, was pitched into a lake on the Alps mountains. Now, listen to the job that 'tis mine to perform on the night of ivery Good Friday. The ould divil goes down in the pool and drags up Pontius, and the water is bilin' and spewin' like a wash pot. And the ould divil sets the body on top of a throne on the rocks, and thin comes me share of the job. Oh, sir, ye would pity me thin–ye would pray for the poor Wandering Jew that niver was a Jew if ye could see the horror of the thing that I must do. 'Tis I that must fetch a bowl of water and kneel down before it till it washes its hands. I declare to ye that Pontius Pilate, a man dead two hundred years, dragged up with the lake slime coverin' him and fishes wrigglin' inside of him widout eyes, and in the discomposition of the body, sits there, sir, and washes his hands in the bowl I hold for him on Good Fridays. 'Twas so commanded."

Clearly, the matter had progressed far beyond the scope of the Bugle's local column. There might have been employment here for the alienist or for those who circulate the pledge; but I had had enough of it. I got up, and repeated that I must go.

At this he seized my coat, groveled upon my desk, and burst again into distressful weeping. Whatever it was about, I said to myself that his grief was genuine.

"Come now, Mr. Ader," I said, soothingly; "what is the matter?"

The answer came brokenly through his racking sobs:

"Because I would not . . . let the poor Christ . . . rest . . . upon the step."

His hallucination seemed beyond all reasonable answer; yet the effect of it upon him scarcely merited disrespect. But I knew nothing that might assuage it; and I told him once more that both of us should be leaving the office at once.

Obedient at last, he raised himself from my disheveled desk, and permitted me to half lift him to the floor. The gale of his grief had blown away his words; his freshet of tears had soaked away the crust of his grief. Reminiscence died in him—at least, the coherent part of it.

"'Twas me that did it," he muttered, as I led him toward the door—"me, the shoemaker of Jerusalem."

I got him to the sidewalk, and in the augmented light I saw that his face was seared and lined and warped by a sadness almost incredibly the product of a single lifetime.

And then high up in the firmamental darkness we heard the clamant cries of some great, passing birds. My Wandering Jew lifted his hand, with side-tilted head.

"The Seven Whistlers!" he said, as one introduces well-known friends.

"Wild geese," said I; "but I confess that their number is beyond me."

"They follow me everywhere," he said. "'Twas so commanded. What ye hear is the souls of the seven Jews that helped with the Crucifixion. Sometimes they're plovers and sometimes geese, but ye'll find them always flyin' where I go."

I stood, uncertain how to take my leave. I looked down the street, shuffled my feet, looked back again—and felt my hair rise. The old man had disappeared.

And then my capillaries relaxed, for I dimly saw him footing it away through the darkness. But he walked so swiftly and silently and contrary to the gait promised by his age that my composure was not all restored, though I knew not why.

That night I was foolish enough to take down some dust-covered volumes from my modest shelves. I searched "Hermippus Redivvus" and "Salathiel" and the "Pepys Collection" in vain. And then in a book called "The Citizen of the World," and in one two centuries old, I came upon what I desired. Michob Ader had indeed come to Paris in the year 1643, and related to the Turkish Spy an extraordinary story. He claimed to be the Wandering Jew, and that—

But here I fell asleep, for my editorial duties had not been light that day.

Judge Hoover was the Bugle's candidate for congress. Having to confer with him, I sought his home early the next morning; and we walked together down town through a little street with which I was unfamiliar.

"Did you ever hear of Michob Ader?" I asked him, smiling.

"Why, yes," said the judge. "And that reminds me of my shoes he has for mending. Here is his shop now."

Judge Hoover stepped into a dingy, small shop. I looked up at the sign, and saw "Mike O'Bader, Boot and Shoe Maker," on it. Some wild geese passed above, honking clearly. I scratched my ear and frowned, and then trailed into the shop.

There sat my Wandering Jew on his shoemaker's bench, trimming a half-sole. He was drabbled with dew, grass-stained, unkempt, and miserable; and on his face was still the unexplained wretchedness, the problematic sorrow, the esoteric woe, that had been written there by nothing less, it seemed, than the stylus of the centuries.

Judge Hoover inquired kindly concerning his shoes. The old shoemaker looked up, and spoke sanely enough. He had been ill, he said, for a few days. The next day the shoes would be ready. He looked at me, and I could see that I had no place in his memory. So out we went, and on our way.

"Old Mike," remarked the candidate, "has been on one of his sprees. He gets crazy drunk regularly once a month. But he's a good shoemaker."

"What is his history?" I inquired.

"Whiskey," epitomized Judge Hoover. "That explains him."

I was silent, but I did not accept the explanation. And so, when I had the chance, I asked old man Sellers, who browsed daily on my exchanges.

"Mike O'Bader," said he, "was makin' shoes in Montopolis when I come here goin' on fifteen year ago. I guess whiskey's his trouble. Once a month he gets off the track, and stays so a week. He's got a rigmarole somethin' about his bein' a Jew pedler that he tells ev'rybody. Nobody won't listen to him anymore. When he's sober he ain't sich a fool–he's got a sight of books in the back room of his shop that he reads. I guess you can lay all his trouble to whiskey."

But again I would not. Not yet was my Wandering Jew rightly construed for me. I trust that women may not be allowed a title to all the curiosity in the world. So when Montopolis's oldest inhabitant (some ninety score years younger than Michob Ader) dropped in to acquire promulgation in print, I siphoned his perpetual trickle of reminiscence in the direction of the uninterpreted maker of shoes.

Uncle Abner was the Complete History of Montopolis, bound in butternut.

"O'Bader," he quavered, "come here in '69. He was the first shoemaker in the place. Folks generally considers him crazy at times now. But he don't harm nobody. I s'pose drinkin' upset his mind–yes, drinkin' very likely done it. It's a powerful bad thing, drinkin'. I'm an old, old man, sir, and I never see no good in drinkin'."

I felt disappointment. I was willing to admit drink in the case of my shoemaker, but I preferred it as a recourse instead of a cause. Why had he pitched upon his perpetual, strange note of the Wandering Jew? Why his unutterable grief during his aberration? I could not yet accept whiskey as an explanation.

"Did Mike O'Bader ever have a great loss or trouble of any kind?" I asked.

"Lemme see! About thirty year ago there was somethin' of the kind, I recollect. Montopolis, sir, in them days used to be a mighty strict place.

"Well, Mike O'Bader had a daughter then–a right pretty girl. She was too gay a sort for Montopolis, so one day she slips off to another town and runs away with a circus. It was two years before she comes back, all fixed up in fine clothes and rings and jewelry, to see Mike. He wouldn't have nothin' to do with her, so she stays around town awhile, anyway. I reckon the men folks wouldn't have raised no objections, but the women egged 'em on to order her to leave town. But she had plenty of spunk, and told 'em to mind their own business.

"So one night they decided to run her away. A crowd of men and women drove her out of her house, and chased her with sticks and stones. She run to her father's door, callin' for help. Mike opens it, and when he sees who it is he hits her with his fist and knocks her down and shuts the door.

"And then the crowd kept on chunkin' her till she run clear out of town. And the next day they finds her drowned dead in Hunter's millpond. I mind it all now. That was thirty year ago."

I leaned back in my non-rotary revolving chair and nodded gently, like a mandarin, at my paste-pot.

"When old Mike has a spell," went on Uncle Abner, tepidly garrulous, "he thinks he's the Wanderin' Jew."

"He is," said I, nodding away.

And Uncle Abner cackled insinuatingly at the editor's remark, for he was expecting at least a "stickful" in the "Personal Notes" of the Bugle.

The Duplicity *of* Hargraves

hen Major Pendleton Talbot, of Mobile, sir, and his daughter, Miss Lydia Talbot, came to Washington to reside, they selected for a boarding place a house that stood fifty yards back from one of the quietest avenues. It was an old-fashioned brick building, with a portico upheld by tall white pillars. Stately locusts and elms shaded the yard, and a catalpa tree in season rained its pink and white blossoms upon the grass. Rows of high box bushes lined the fence and walks. It was the Southern style and aspect of the place that pleased the eyes of the Talbots.

In this pleasant, private boarding house they engaged rooms, including a study for Major Talbot, who was adding the finishing chapters to his book, "Anecdotes and Reminiscences of the Alabama Army, Bench, and Bar."

Major Talbot was of the old, old South. The present day had little interest or excellence in his eyes. His mind lived in that period before the Civil War, when the Talbots owned thousands of acres of fine cotton land and the slaves to till them; when the family mansion was the scene of princely hospitality, and drew its guests from the aristocracy of the South. Out of that period he had brought all its old pride and scruples of honor, an antiquated and punctilious politeness, and (you would think) its wardrobe.

Such clothes were surely never made within fifty years. The major was tall, but whenever he made that wonderful, archaic genuflexion he called a bow, the corners of his frock coat swept the floor. That garment was a surprise even to Washington, which has long ago ceased to shy at the frocks and broad-brimmed hats of Southern congressmen. One of the boarders christened it a "Father Hubbard," and it certainly was high in the waist and full in the skirt.

But the major, with all his queer clothes, his immense area of plaited, raveling shirt bosom, and the little black string tie with the bow always slipping on one side, both was smiled at and liked in Mrs. Vardeman's select boarding house. Some of the young department clerks would often "string him," as they called it, getting him started upon the subject dearest to him–the traditions and history of his beloved Southland. During his talks he would quote freely from the "Anecdotes and Reminiscences." But they were very careful not to let him see their designs, for in spite of his sixty-eight years, he could make the boldest of them uncomfortable under the steady regard of his piercing gray eyes.

Miss Lydia was a plump, little old maid of thirty-five, with smoothly drawn, tightly twisted hair that made her look still older. Old fashioned, too, she was; but ante-bellum glory did not radiate from her as it did from the major. She possessed a thrifty common sense; and it was she who handled the finances of the family, and met all comers when there were bills to pay. The major regarded board bills and wash bills as contemptible nuisances. They kept coming in so persistently and so often. Why, the major wanted to know, could they not be filed and paid in a lump sum at some convenient period–say when the "Anecdotes and Reminiscences" had been published and paid for? Miss Lydia would calmly go on with her sewing and say, "We'll pay as we go as long as the money lasts, and then perhaps they'll have to lump it."

Most of Mrs. Vardeman's boarders were away during the day, being nearly all department clerks and businessmen; but there was one of them who was about the house a great deal from morning to night. This was a young man named Henry Hopkins Hargraves–everyone in the house addressed him by his full name–who was engaged at one of the popular vaudeville theatres. Vaudeville has risen to such a respectable plane in the last few years, and Mr. Hargraves was such a modest and well-mannered person, that Mrs. Vardeman could find no objection to enrolling him upon her list of boarders.

At the theatre Hargraves was known as an all-round dialect comedian, having a large repertoire of German, Irish, Swede, and blackface specialties. But Mr. Hargraves was ambitious, and often spoke of his great desire to succeed in legitimate comedy.

This young man appeared to conceive a strong fancy for Major Talbot. Whenever that gentleman would begin his Southern reminiscences, or repeat some of the liveliest of the anecdotes, Hargraves could always be found, the most attentive among his listeners.

For a time the major showed an inclination to discourage the advances of the "play actor," as he privately termed him; but soon the young man's agreeable manner and indubitable appreciation of the old gentleman's stories completely won him over.

It was not long before the two were like old chums. The major set apart each afternoon to read to him the manuscript of his book. During the anecdotes Hargraves never failed to laugh at exactly the right point. The major was moved to declare to Miss Lydia one day that young Hargraves possessed remarkable perception and a gratifying respect for the old regime. And when it came to talking of those old days– if Major Talbot liked to talk, Mr. Hargraves was entranced to listen.

Like almost all old people who talk of the past, the major loved to linger over details. In describing the splendid, almost royal, days of the old planters, he would hesitate until he had recalled the name of the Negro who held his horse, or the exact date of certain minor happenings, or the number of bales of cotton raised in such a year; but Hargraves never grew impatient or lost interest. On the contrary, he would advance questions on a variety of subjects connected with the life of that time, and he never failed to extract ready replies.

The fox hunts, the 'possum suppers, the hoe downs and jubilees in the Negro quarters, the banquets in the plantation-house hall, when invitations went for fifty miles around; the occasional feuds with the neighboring gentry; the major's duel with Rathbone Culbertson about Kitty Chalmers, who afterward married a Thwaite of South Carolina; and private yacht races for fabulous sums on Mobile Bay; the quaint beliefs, improvident habits, and loyal virtues of the old slaves–all these were subjects that held both the major and Hargraves absorbed for hours at a time.

Sometimes, at night, when the young man would be coming upstairs to his room after his turn at the theatre was over, the major would appear at the door of his study and beckon archly to him. Going in, Hargraves would find a little table set with a decanter, sugar bowl, fruit, and a big bunch of fresh green mint.

"It occurred to me," the major would begin–he was always ceremonious– "that perhaps you might have found your duties at the–at your place of occupation– sufficiently arduous to enable you, Mr. Hargraves, to appreciate what the poet might well have had in his mind when he wrote, 'tired Nature's sweet restorer,'–one of our Southern juleps."

It was a fascination to Hargraves to watch him make it. He took rank among artists when he began, and he never varied the process. With what delicacy he bruised the mint; with what exquisite nicety he estimated the ingredients; with what solicitous care he capped the compound with the scarlet fruit glowing against the dark green fringe! And then the hospitality and grace with which he offered it, after the selected oat straws had been plunged into its tinkling depths!

After about four months in Washington, Miss Lydia discovered one morning that they were almost without money. The "Anecdotes and Reminiscences" was completed, but publishers had not jumped at the collected gems of Alabama sense and wit. The rental of a small house which they still owned in Mobile was two months in arrears. Their board money for the month would be due in three days. Miss Lydia called her father to a consultation.

"No money?" said he with a surprised look. "It is quite annoying to be called on so frequently for these petty sums. Really, I–"

The major searched his pockets. He found only a two-dollar bill, which he returned to his vest pocket.

"I must attend to this at once, Lydia," he said. "Kindly get me my umbrella and I will go down town immediately. The congressman from our district, General Fulghum, assured me some days ago that he would use his influence to get my book published at an early date. I will go to his hotel at once and see what arrangement has been made."

With a sad little smile Miss Lydia watched him button his "Father Hubbard" and depart, pausing at the door, as he always did, to bow profoundly.

That evening, at dark, he returned. It seemed that Congressman Fulghum had seen the publisher who had the major's manuscript for reading. That person had said that if the anecdotes, etc., were carefully pruned down about one half, in order to eliminate the sectional and class prejudice with which the book was dyed from end to end, he might consider its publication.

The major was in a white heat of anger, but regained his equanimity, according to his code of manners, as soon as he was in Miss Lydia's presence.

"We must have money," said Miss Lydia, with a little wrinkle above her nose. "Give me the two dollars, and I will telegraph to Uncle Ralph for some tonight."

The major drew a small envelope from his upper vest pocket and tossed it on the table.

"Perhaps it was injudicious," he said mildly, "but the sum was so merely nominal that I bought tickets to the theatre tonight. It's a new war drama, Lydia. I thought you would be pleased to witness its first production in Washington. I am told that the South has very fair treatment in the play. I confess I should like to see the performance myself."

Miss Lydia threw up her hands in silent despair.

Still, as the tickets were bought, they might as well be used. So that evening, as they sat in the theatre listening to the lively overture, even Miss Lydia was minded to relegate their troubles, for the hour, to second place. The major, in spotless linen, with his extraordinary coat showing only where it was closely buttoned, and his white hair smoothly roached, looked really fine and distinguished. The curtain went up on the first act of "A Magnolia Flower," revealing a typical Southern plantation scene. Major Talbot betrayed some interest.

"Oh, see!" exclaimed Miss Lydia, nudging his arm, and pointing to her program.

The major put on his glasses and read the line in the cast of characters that her finger indicated.

Col. Webster Calhoun .... H. Hopkins Hargraves.

"It's our Mr. Hargraves," said Miss Lydia. "It must be his first appearance in what he calls 'the legitimate.' I'm so glad for him."

Not until the second act did Col. Webster Calhoun appear upon the stage. When he made his entry Major Talbot gave an audible sniff, glared at him, and seemed to freeze solid. Miss Lydia uttered a little, ambiguous squeak and crumpled her program in her hand. For Colonel Calhoun was made up as nearly resembling Major Talbot as one pea does another. The long, thin white hair, curly at the ends, the aristocratic beak of a nose, the crumpled, wide, raveling shirtfront, the string tie, with the bow nearly under one ear, were almost exactly duplicated. And then, to clinch the imitation, he wore the twin to the major's supposed to be unparalleled coat. High-collared, baggy, empire-waisted, ample-skirted, hanging a foot lower in front than behind, the garment could have been designed from no other pattern. From then on, the major and Miss Lydia sat bewitched, and saw the counterfeit presentment of a haughty Talbot "dragged," as the major afterward expressed it, "through the slanderous mire of a corrupt stage."

Mr. Hargraves had used his opportunities well. He had caught the major's little idiosyncrasies of speech, accent, and intonation and his pompous courtliness to perfection–exaggerating all to the purposes of the stage. When he performed that marvelous bow that the major fondly imagined to be the pink of all salutations, the audience sent forth a sudden round of hearty applause.

Miss Lydia sat immovable, not daring to glance toward her father. Sometimes her hand next to him would be laid against her cheek, as if to conceal the smile which, in spite of her disapproval, she could not entirely suppress.

The culmination of Hargraves's audacious imitation took place in the third act. The scene is where Colonel Calhoun entertains a few of the neighboring planters in his "den."

Standing at a table in the center of the stage, with his friends grouped about him, he delivers that inimitable, rambling, character monologue so famous in "A Magnolia Flower," at the same time that he deftly makes juleps for the party.

Major Talbot, sitting quietly, but white with indignation, heard his best stories retold, his pet theories and hobbies advanced and expanded, and the dream of the "Anecdotes and Reminiscences" served, exaggerated and garbled. His favorite narrative–that of his duel with Rathbone Culbertson–was not omitted, and it was delivered with more fire, egotism, and gusto than the major himself put into it.

The monologue concluded with a quaint, delicious, witty little lecture on the art of concocting a julep, illustrated by the act. Here Major Talbot's delicate but showy science was reproduced to a hair's breadth–from his dainty handling of the fragrant weed–"the one-thousandth part of a grain too much pressure, gentlemen, and you extract the bitterness, instead of the aroma, of this heaven-bestowed plant"–to his solicitous selection of the oaten straws.

At the close of the scene the audience raised a tumultuous roar of appreciation. The portrayal of the type was so exact, so sure and thorough, that the leading characters in the play were forgotten. After repeated calls, Hargraves came before the curtain and bowed, his rather boyish face bright and flushed with the knowledge of success.

At last Miss Lydia turned and looked at the major. His thin nostrils were working like the gills of a fish. He laid both shaking hands upon the arms of his chair to rise.

"We will go, Lydia," he said chokingly. "This is an abominable– desecration."

Before he could rise, she pulled him back into his seat. "We will stay it out," she declared. "Do you want to advertise the copy by exhibiting the original coat?" So they remained to the end.

Hargraves's success must have kept him up late that night, for neither at the breakfast nor at the dinner table did he appear.

About three in the afternoon he tapped at the door of Major Talbot's study. The major opened it, and Hargraves walked in with his hands full of the morning papers– too full of his triumph to notice anything unusual in the major's demeanor.

"I put it all over 'em last night, major," he began exultantly. "I had my inning, and, I think, scored. Here's what the Post says:

His conception and portrayal of the old-time Southern colonel, with his absurd grandiloquence, his eccentric garb, his quaint idioms and phrases, his moth-eaten pride of family, and his really kind heart, fastidious sense of honor, and lovable simplicity, is the best delineation of a character role on the boards today. The coat worn by Colonel Calhoun is itself nothing less than an evolution of genius. Mr. Hargraves has captured his public.

"How does that sound, major, for a first nighter?"

"I had the honor"–the major's voice sounded ominously frigid–"of witnessing your very remarkable performance, sir, last night."

Hargraves looked disconcerted.

"You were there? I didn't know you ever–I didn't know you cared for the theatre. Oh, I say, Major Talbot," he exclaimed frankly, "don't you be offended. I admit I did get a lot of pointers from you that helped me out wonderfully in the part. But it's a type, you know–not individual. The way the audience caught on shows that. Half the patrons of that theatre are Southerners. They recognized it."

"Mr. Hargraves," said the major, who had remained standing, "you have put upon me an unpardonable insult. You have burlesqued my person, grossly betrayed my confidence, and misused my hospitality. If I thought you possessed the faintest conception of what is the sign manual of a gentleman, or what is due one, I would call you out, sir, old as I am. I will ask you to leave the room, sir."

The actor appeared to be slightly bewildered, and seemed hardly to take in the full meaning of the old gentleman's words.

"I am truly sorry you took offence," he said regretfully. "Up here we don't look at things just as you people do. I know men who would buy out half the house to have their personality put on the stage so the public would recognize it."

"They are not from Alabama, sir," said the major haughtily.

"Perhaps not. I have a pretty good memory, major; let me quote a few lines from your book. In response to a toast at a banquet given in-- Milledgeville, I believe--you uttered, and intend to have printed, these words:

The Northern man is utterly without sentiment or warmth except in so far as the feelings may be turned to his own commercial profit. He will suffer without resentment any imputation cast upon the honor of himself or his loved ones that does not bear with it the consequence of pecuniary loss. In his charity, he gives with a liberal hand; but it must be heralded with the trumpet and chronicled in brass.

"Do you think that picture is fairer than the one you saw of Colonel Calhoun last night?"

"The description," said the major frowning, "is--not without grounds. Some exag-- latitude must be allowed in public speaking."

"And in public acting," replied Hargraves.

"That is not the point," persisted the major, unrelenting. "It was a personal caricature. I positively decline to overlook it, sir."

"Major Talbot," said Hargraves, with a winning smile, "I wish you would understand me. I want you to know that I never dreamed of insulting you. In my profession, all life belongs to me. I take what I want, and what I can, and return it over the footlights. Now, if you will, let's let it go at that. I came in to see you about something else. We've been pretty good friends for some months, and I'm going to take the risk of offending you again. I know you are hard up for money--never mind how I found out; a boarding house is no place to keep such matters secret--and I want you to let me help you out of the pinch. I've been there often enough myself. I've been getting a fair salary all the season, and I've saved some money. You're welcome to a couple hundred-- or even more--until you get--"

"Stop!" commanded the major, with his arm outstretched. "It seems that my book didn't lie, after all. You think your money salve will heal all the hurts of honor. Under no circumstances would I accept a loan from a casual acquaintance; and as to you, sir, I would starve before I would consider your insulting offer of a financial adjustment of the circumstances we have discussed. I beg to repeat my request relative to your quitting the apartment."

Hargraves took his departure without another word. He also left the house the same day, moving, as Mrs. Vardeman explained at the supper table, nearer the vicinity of the down-town theatre, where "A Magnolia Flower" was booked for a week's run.

Critical was the situation with Major Talbot and Miss Lydia. There was no one in Washington to whom the major's scruples allowed him to apply for a loan. Miss Lydia wrote a letter to Uncle Ralph, but it was doubtful whether that relative's constricted affairs would permit him to furnish help. The major was forced to make an apologetic address to Mrs. Vardeman regarding the delayed payment for board, referring to "delinquent rentals" and "delayed remittances" in a rather confused strain.

Deliverance came from an entirely unexpected source.

Late one afternoon the door maid came up and announced an old colored man who wanted to see Major Talbot. The major asked that he be sent up to his study. Soon an old darkey appeared in the doorway, with his hat in hand, bowing, and scraping with one clumsy foot. He was quite decently dressed in a baggy suit of black. His big, coarse shoes shone with a metallic luster suggestive of stove polish. His bushy wool was gray–almost white. After middle life, it is difficult to estimate the age of a Negro. This one might have seen as many years as had Major Talbot.

"I be bound you don't know me, Mars' Pendleton," were his first words.

The major rose and came forward at the old, familiar style of address. It was one of the old plantation darkeys without a doubt; but they had been widely scattered, and he could not recall the voice or face.

"I don't believe I do," he said kindly–"unless you will assist my memory."

"Don't you 'member Cindy's Mose, Mars' Pendleton, what 'migrated 'mediately after de war?"

"Wait a moment," said the major, rubbing his forehead with the tips of his fingers. He loved to recall everything connected with those beloved days. "Cindy's Mose," he reflected. "You worked among the horses–breaking the colts. Yes, I remember now. After the surrender, you took the name of–don't prompt me–Mitchell, and went to the West–to Nebraska."

"Yassir, yassir,"–the old man's face stretched with a delighted grin–"dat's him, dat's it. Newbraska. Dat's me–Mose Mitchell. Old Uncle Mose Mitchell, dey calls me now. Old mars', your pa, gimme a pah of dem mule colts when I lef' fur to staht me goin' with. You 'member dem colts, Mars' Pendleton?"

"I don't seem to recall the colts," said the major. "You know I was married the first year of the war and living at the old Follinsbee place. But sit down, sit down, Uncle Mose. I'm glad to see you. I hope you have prospered."

Uncle Mose took a chair and laid his hat carefully on the floor beside it.

"Yassir; of late I done mouty famous. When I first got to Newbraska, dey folks come all roun' me to see dem mule colts. Dey ain't see no mules like dem in Newbraska. I sold dem mules for three hundred dollars. Yassir–three hundred.

"Den I open a blacksmith shop, suh, and made some money and bought some lan'. Me and my old 'oman done raised up seb'm chillun, and all doin' well 'cept two of 'em what died. Fo' year ago a railroad come along and staht a town slam ag'inst my lan', and, suh, Mars' Pendleton, Uncle Mose am worth leb'm thousand dollars in money, property, and lan'."

"I'm glad to hear it," said the major heartily. "Glad to hear it."

"And dat little baby of yo'n, Mars' Pendleton–one what you name Miss Lyddy–I be bound dat little tad done growed up tell nobody wouldn't know her."

The major stepped to the door and called: "Lydia, dear, will you come?"

Miss Lydia, looking quite grown up and a little worried, came in from her room.

"Dar, now! What'd I tell you? I knowed dat baby done be plum growed up. You don't 'member Uncle Mose, child?"

"This is Aunt Cindy's Mose, Lydia," explained the major. "He left Sunnymead for the West when you were two years old."

"Well," said Miss Lydia, "I can hardly be expected to remember you, Uncle Mose, at that age. And, as you say, I'm 'plum growed up,' and was a blessed long time ago. But I'm glad to see you, even if I can't remember you."

And she was. And so was the major. Something alive and tangible had come to link them with the happy past. The three sat and talked over the olden times, the major and Uncle Mose correcting or prompting each other as they reviewed the plantation scenes and days.

The major inquired what the old man was doing so far from his home.

"Uncle Mose am a delicate," he explained, "to de grand Baptis' convention in dis city. I never preached none, but bein' a residin' elder in de church, and able fur to pay my own expenses, dey sent me along."

"And how did you know we were in Washington?" inquired Miss Lydia.

"Dey's a cullud man works in de hotel whar I stops, what comes from Mobile. He told me he seen Mars' Pendleton comin' outen dish here house one mawnin'.

"What I come fur," continued Uncle Mose, reaching into his pocket– "besides de sight of home folks–was to pay Mars' Pendleton what I owes him."

"Owe me?" said the major, in surprise.

"Yassir–three hundred dollars." He handed the major a roll of bills. "When I lef' old mars' says: 'Take dem mule colts, Mose, and, if it be so you gits able, pay fur 'em'. Yassir–dem was his words. De war had done lef' old mars' po' hisself. Old mars' bein' 'long ago dead, de debt descends to Mars' Pendleton. Three hundred dollars. Uncle Mose is plenty able to pay now. When dat railroad buy my lan' I laid off to pay fur dem mules. Count de money, Mars' Pendleton. Dat's what I sold dem mules fur. Yassir."

Tears were in Major Talbot's eyes. He took Uncle Mose's hand and laid his other upon his shoulder.

"Dear, faithful, old servitor," he said in an unsteady voice, "I don't mind saying to you that 'Mars' Pendleton' spent his last dollar in the world a week ago. We will accept this money, Uncle Mose, since, in a way, it is a sort of payment, as well as a token of the loyalty and devotion of the old regime. Lydia, my dear, take the money. You are better fitted than I to manage its expenditure."

"Take it, honey," said Uncle Mose. "Hit belongs to you. Hit's Talbot money."

After Uncle Mose had gone, Miss Lydia had a good cry–for joy; and the major turned his face to a corner, and smoked his clay pipe volcanically.

The succeeding days saw the Talbots restored to peace and ease. Miss Lydia's face lost its worried look. The major appeared in a new frock coat, in which he looked like a wax figure personifying the memory of his golden age. Another publisher who read the manuscript of the "Anecdotes and Reminiscences" thought that, with a little retouching and toning down of the high lights, he could make a really bright and salable volume of it. Altogether, the situation was comfortable, and not without the touch of hope that is often sweeter than arrived blessings.

One day, about a week after their piece of good luck, a maid brought a letter for Miss Lydia to her room. The postmark showed that it was from New York. Not knowing any one there, Miss Lydia, in a mild flutter of wonder, sat down by her table and opened the letter with her scissors. This was what she read:

Dear Miss Talbot:

I thought you might be glad to learn of my good fortune. I have received and accepted an offer of two hundred dollars per week by a New York stock company to play Colonel Calhoun in "A Magnolia Flower."

There is something else I wanted you to know. I guess you'd better not tell Major Talbot. I was anxious to make him some amends for the great help he was to me in studying the part, and for the bad humor he was in about it. He refused to let me, so I did it anyhow. I could easily spare the three hundred.

Sincerely yours,
H. Hopkins Hargraves,
P.S. How did I play Uncle Mose?

Major Talbot, passing through the hall, saw Miss Lydia's door open and stopped.
"Any mail for us this morning, Lydia, dear?" he asked.
Miss Lydia slid the letter beneath a fold of her dress.
"The Mobile Chronicle came," she said promptly. "It's on the table in your study."

Let Me Feel Your Pulse

o I went to a doctor.

"How long has it been since you took any alcohol into your system?" he asked.

Turning my head sidewise, I answered, "Oh, quite a while."

He was a young doctor, somewhere between twenty and forty. He wore heliotrope socks, but he looked like Napoleon. I liked him immensely.

"Now," said he, "I am going to show you the effect of alcohol upon your circulation." I think it was "circulation" he said; though it may have been "advertising."

He bared my left arm to the elbow, brought out a bottle of whiskey, and gave me a drink. He began to look more like Napoleon. I began to like him better.

Then he put a tight compress on my upper arm, stopped my pulse with his fingers, and squeezed a rubber bulb connected with an apparatus on a stand that looked like a thermometer. The mercury jumped up and down without seeming to stop anywhere; but the doctor said it registered two hundred and thirty-seven or one hundred and sixty-five or some such number.

"Now," said he, "you see what alcohol does to the blood-pressure."

"It's marvelous," said I, "but do you think it a sufficient test? Have one on me, and let's try the other arm." But, no!

Then he grasped my hand. I thought I was doomed and he was saying good-bye. But all he wanted to do was to jab a needle into the end of a finger and compare the red drop with a lot of fifty-cent poker chips that he had fastened to a card.

"It's the hemoglobin test," he explained. "The color of your blood is wrong."

"Well," said I, "I know it should be blue; but this is a country of mix-ups. Some of my ancestors were cavaliers; but they got thick with some people on Nantucket Island, so–"

"I mean," said the doctor, "that the shade of red is too light."

"Oh," said I, "it's a case of matching instead of matches."

The doctor then pounded me severely in the region of the chest. When he did that, I don't know whether he reminded me most of Napoleon or Battling or Lord Nelson. Then he looked grave and mentioned a string of grievances that the flesh is heir to– mostly ending in *itis*. I immediately paid him fifteen dollars on account.

"Is or are it or some or any of them necessarily fatal?" I asked. I thought my connection with the matter justified my manifesting a certain amount of interest.

"All of them," he answered cheerfully. "But their progress may be arrested. With care and proper continuous treatment you may live to be eighty-five or ninety."

I began to think of the doctor's bill. "Eighty-five would be sufficient, I am sure," was my comment. I paid him ten dollars more on account.

"The first thing to do," he said, with renewed animation, "is to find a sanitarium where you will get a complete rest for a while, and allow your nerves to get into a better condition. I myself will go with you and select a suitable one."

So he took me to a madhouse in the Catskills. It was on a bare mountain frequented only by infrequent frequenters. You could see nothing but stones and boulders; some patches of snow, and scattered pine trees. The young physician in charge was most agreeable. He gave me a stimulant without applying a compress to the arm. It was luncheon time, and we were invited to partake. There were about twenty inmates at little tables in the dining room. The young physician in charge came to our table and said: "It is a custom with our guests not to regard themselves as patients, but merely as tired ladies and gentlemen taking a rest. Whatever slight maladies they may have are never alluded to in conversation."

My doctor called loudly to a waitress to bring some phosphoglycerate of lime hash, dog-bread, bromo-seltzer pancakes, and *nux vomica* tea for my repast. Then a sound arose like a sudden windstorm among pine trees. It was produced by every guest in the room whispering loudly, "Neurasthenia!"– except one man with a nose, whom I distinctly heard say, "Chronic alcoholism." I hope to meet him again. The physician in charge turned and walked away.

An hour or so after luncheon he conducted us to the workshop–say fifty yards from the house. Thither the guests had been conducted by the physician in charge's understudy and sponge-holder–a man with feet and a blue sweater. He was so tall that I was not sure he had a face; but the Armour Packing Company would have been delighted with his hands.

"Here," said the physician in charge, "our guests find relaxation from past mental worries by devoting themselves to physical labor–recreation, in reality."

There were turning-lathes, carpenters' outfits, clay-modeling tools, spinning-wheels, weaving-frames, treadmills, bass drums, enlarged-crayon-portrait apparatuses, blacksmith forges, and everything, seemingly, that could interest the paying lunatic guests of a first-rate sanitarium.

"The lady making mud pies in the corner," whispered the physician in charge, "is no other than–Lula Lulington, the authoress of the novel entitled 'Why Love Loves.' What she is doing now is simply to rest her mind after performing that piece of work."

I had seen the book. "Why doesn't she do it by writing another one instead?" I asked.

As you see, I wasn't as far gone as they thought I was.

"The gentleman pouring water through the funnel," continued the physician in charge, "is a Wall Street broker broken down from overwork."

I buttoned my coat.

Others he pointed out were architects playing with Noah's arks, ministers reading Darwin's "Theory of Evolution," lawyers sawing wood, tired-out society ladies talking Ibsen to the blue-sweatered sponge-holder, a neurotic millionaire lying asleep on the floor, and a prominent artist drawing a little red wagon around the room.

"You look pretty strong," said the physician in charge to me. "I think the best mental relaxation for you would be throwing small boulders over the mountainside and then bringing them up again."

I was a hundred yards away before my doctor overtook me.

"What's the matter?" he asked.

"The matter is," said I, "that there are no airplanes handy. So I am going to merrily and hastily jog the foot-pathway to yon station and catch the first unlimited-soft-coal express back to town."

"Well," said the doctor, "perhaps you are right. This seems hardly the suitable place for you. But what you need is rest–absolute rest and exercise."

That night I went to a hotel in the city, and said to the clerk: "What I need is absolute rest and exercise. Can you give me a room with one of those tall folding beds in it, and a relay of bellboys to work it up and down while I rest?"

The clerk rubbed a speck off one of his fingernails and glanced sidewise at a tall man in a white hat sitting in the lobby. That man came over and asked me politely if I had seen the shrubbery at the west entrance. I had not, so he showed it to me and then looked me over.

"I thought you had 'em," he said, not unkindly, "but I guess you're all right. You'd better go see a doctor, old man."

A week afterward my doctor tested my blood pressure again without the preliminary stimulant. He looked to me a little less like Napoleon. And his socks were of a shade of tan that did not appeal to me.

"What you need," he decided, "is sea air and companionship."

"Would a mermaid–" I began; but he slipped on his professional manner.

"I myself," he said, "will take you to the Hotel Bonair off the coast of Long Island and see that you get in good shape. It is a quiet, comfortable resort where you will soon recuperate."

The Hotel Bonair proved to be a nine-hundred-room fashionable hostelry on an island off the main shore. Everybody who did not dress for dinner was shoved into a side dining room and given only a terrapin and champagne *table d'hote.*[2] The bay was a great stamping ground for wealthy yachtsmen. The Corsair anchored there the day we arrived. I saw Mr. Morgan standing on deck eating a cheese sandwich and gazing longingly at the hotel. Still, it was a very inexpensive place. Nobody could afford to pay their prices. When you went away you simply left your baggage, stole a skiff, and beat it for the mainland in the night.

When I had been there one day I got a pad of monogrammed telegraph blanks at the clerk's desk and began to wire to all my friends for get-away money. My doctor and I played one game of croquet on the golf links and went to sleep on the lawn.

When we got back to town a thought seemed to occur to him suddenly. "By the way," he asked, "how do you feel?"

"Relieved of very much," I replied.

Now a consulting physician is different. He isn't exactly sure whether he is to be paid or not, and this uncertainty insures you either the most careful or the most careless attention. My doctor took me to see a consulting physician. He made a poor guess and gave me careful attention. I liked him immensely. He put me through some coordination exercises.

"Have you a pain in the back of your head?" he asked. I told him I had not.

"Shut your eyes," he ordered, "put your feet close together, and jump backward as far as you can."

---

[2] *A restaurant meal offered at a fixed price and with few if any choices -*

I always was a good backward jumper with my eyes shut, so I obeyed. My head struck the edge of the bathroom door, which had been left open and was only three feet away. The doctor was very sorry. He had overlooked the fact that the door was open. He closed it.

"Now touch your nose with your right forefinger," he said.

"Where is it?" I asked.

"On your face," said he.

"I mean my right forefinger," I explained.

"Oh, excuse me," said he. He reopened the bathroom door, and I took my finger out of the crack of it. After I had performed the marvelous digito-nasal feat I said:

"I do not wish to deceive you as to symptoms, Doctor; I really have something like a pain in the back of my head." He ignored the symptom and examined my heart carefully with a latest-popular-air-penny-in-the-slot ear-trumpet. I felt like a ballad.

"Now," he said, "gallop like a horse for about five minutes around the room."

I gave the best imitation I could of a disqualified Percheron being led out of Madison Square Garden. Then, without dropping in a penny, he listened to my chest again.

"No glanders in our family, Doc," I said.

The consulting physician held up his forefinger within three inches of my nose. "Look at my finger," he commanded.

"Did you ever try Pears'–" I began; but he went on with his test rapidly.

"Now look across the bay. At my finger. Across the bay. At my finger. At my finger. Across the bay. Across the bay. At my finger. Across the bay." This for about three minutes.

He explained that this was a test of the action of the brain. It seemed easy to me. I never once mistook his finger for the bay. I'll bet that if he had used the phrases: "Gaze, as it were, unpreoccupied, outward–or rather laterally–in the direction of the horizon, underlaid, so to speak, with the adjacent fluid inlet," and "Now, returning–or rather, in a manner, withdrawing your attention, bestow it upon my upraised digit"– I'll bet, I say, that Henry James himself could have passed the examination.

After asking me if I had ever had a grand uncle with curvature of the spine or a cousin with swelled ankles, the two doctors retired to the bathroom and sat on the edge of the bathtub for their consultation. I ate an apple, and gazed first at my finger and then across the bay.

The doctors came out looking grave. More: they looked tombstones and Tennessee-papers-please-copy. They wrote out a diet list to which I was to be restricted. It had everything that I had ever heard of to eat on it, except snails. And I never eat a snail unless it overtakes me and bites me first.

"You must follow this diet strictly," said the doctors.

"I'd follow it a mile if I could get one-tenth of what's on it," I answered.

"Of next importance," they went on, "is outdoor air and exercise. And here is a prescription that will be of great benefit to you."

Then all of us took something. They took their hats, and I took my departure.

I went to a druggist and showed him the prescription. "It will be $2.87 for an ounce bottle," he said.

"Will you give me a piece of your wrapping cord?" said I.

I made a hole in the prescription, ran the cord through it, tied it around my neck, and tucked it inside. All of us have a little superstition, and mine runs to a confidence in amulets.

Of course there was nothing the matter with me, but I was very ill. I couldn't work, sleep, eat, or bowl. The only way I could get any sympathy was to go without shaving for four days. Even then somebody would say: "Old man, you look as hardy as a pine knot. Been up for a jaunt in the Maine woods, eh?"

Then, suddenly, I remembered that I must have outdoor air and exercise. So I went down South to John's. John is an approximate relative by verdict of a preacher standing with a little book in his hands in a bower of chrysanthemums while a hundred thousand people looked on. John has a country house seven miles from Pineville. It is at an altitude and on the Blue Ridge Mountains in a state too dignified to be dragged into this controversy. John is mica, which is more valuable and clearer than gold.

He met me at Pineville, and we took the trolley car to his home. It is a big, neighborless cottage on a hill surrounded by a hundred mountains. We got off at his little private station, where John's family and Amaryllis met and greeted us. Amaryllis looked at me a trifle anxiously.

A rabbit came bounding across the hill between us and the house. I threw down my suitcase and pursued it hotfoot. After I had run twenty yards and seen it disappear, I sat down on the grass and wept disconsolately.

"I can't catch a rabbit anymore," I sobbed. "I'm of no further use in the world. I may as well be dead."

"Oh, what is it—what is it, Brother John?" I heard Amaryllis say.

"Nerves a little unstrung," said John, in his calm way. "Don't worry. Get up, you rabbit-chaser, and come on to the house before the biscuits get cold." It was about twilight, and the mountains came up nobly to Miss Murfree's descriptions of them.

Soon after dinner I announced that I believed I could sleep for a year or two, including legal holidays. So I was shown to a room as big and cool as a flower garden, where there was a bed as broad as a lawn. Soon afterward the remainder of the household retired, and then there fell upon the land a silence.

I had not heard a silence before in years. It was absolute. I raised myself on my elbow and listened to it. Sleep! I thought that if I only could hear a star twinkle or a blade of grass sharpen itself I could compose myself to rest. I thought once that I heard a sound like the sail of a catboat flapping as it veered about in a breeze, but I decided that it was probably only a tack in the carpet. Still I listened.

Suddenly some belated little bird alighted upon the windowsill, and, in what he no doubt considered sleepy tones, enunciated the noise generally translated as "cheep!"

I leaped into the air.

"Hey! what's the matter down there?" called John from his room above mine.

"Oh, nothing," I answered, "except that I accidentally bumped my head against the ceiling."

The next morning I went out on the porch and looked at the mountains. There were forty-seven of them in sight. I shuddered, went into the big hall sitting room of the house, selected "Pancoast's Family Practice of Medicine" from a bookcase, and began to read. John came in, took the book away from me, and led me outside. He has a farm of three hundred acres furnished with the usual complement of barns, mules, peasantry, and harrows with three front teeth broken off. I had seen such things in my childhood, and my heart began to sink.

Then John spoke of alfalfa, and I brightened at once. "Oh, yes," said I, "wasn't she in the chorus of–let's see–"

"Green, you know," said John, "and tender, and you plow it under after the first season."

"I know," said I, "and the grass grows over her."

"Right," said John. "You know something about farming, after all."

"I know something of some farmers," said I, "and a sure scythe will mow them down some day."

On the way back to the house a beautiful and inexplicable creature walked across our path. I stopped irresistibly fascinated, gazing at it. John waited patiently, smoking his cigarette. He is a modern farmer. After ten minutes he said: "Are you going to stand there looking at that chicken all day? Breakfast is nearly ready."

"A chicken?" said I.

"A White Orpington hen, if you want to particularize."

"A White Orpington hen?" I repeated, with intense interest. The fowl walked slowly away with graceful dignity, and I followed like a child after the Pied Piper. Five minutes more were allowed me by John, and then he took me by the sleeve and conducted me to breakfast.

After I had been there a week I began to grow alarmed. I was sleeping and eating well and actually beginning to enjoy life. For a man in my desperate condition that would never do. So I sneaked down to the trolley-car station, took the car for Pineville, and went to see one of the best physicians in town.

By this time I knew exactly what to do when I needed medical treatment. I hung my hat on the back of a chair, and said rapidly:

"Doctor, I have cirrhosis of the heart, indurated arteries, neurasthenia, neuritis, acute indigestion, and convalescence. I am going to live on a strict diet. I shall also take a tepid bath at night and a cold one in the morning. I shall endeavor to be cheerful, and fix my mind on pleasant subjects. In the way of drugs I intend to take a phosphorous pill three times a day, preferably after meals, and a tonic composed of the tinctures of gentian, cinchona, calisaya, and cardamon compound. Into each teaspoonful of this I shall mix tincture of *nux vomica*, beginning with one drop and increasing it a drop each day until the maximum dose is reached. I shall drop this with a medicine-dropper, which can be procured at a trifling cost at any pharmacy. Good morning."

I took my hat and walked out. After I had closed the door I remembered something that I had forgotten to say. I opened it again. The doctor had not moved from where he had been sitting, but he gave a slightly nervous start when he saw me again.

"I forgot to mention," said I, "that I shall also take absolute rest and exercise."

After this consultation I felt much better. The reestablishing in my mind of the fact that I was hopelessly ill gave me so much satisfaction that I almost became gloomy again. There is nothing more alarming to a neurasthenic than to feel himself growing well and cheerful.

John looked after me carefully. After I had evinced so much interest in his White Orpington chicken he tried his best to divert my mind, and was particular to lock his hen house of nights. Gradually the tonic mountain air, the wholesome food, and the daily walks among the hills so alleviated my malady that I became utterly wretched and despondent. I heard of a country doctor who lived in the mountains nearby. I went to see him and told him the whole story. He was a gray-bearded man with clear, blue, wrinkled eyes, in a homemade suit of gray jeans.

In order to save time I diagnosed my case, touched my nose with my right forefinger, struck myself below the knee to make my foot kick, sounded my chest, stuck out my tongue, and asked him the price of cemetery lots in Pineville.

He lit his pipe and looked at me for about three minutes. "Brother," he said, after a while, "you are in a mighty bad way. There's a chance for you to pull through, but it's a mighty slim one."

"What can it be?" I asked eagerly. "I have taken arsenic and gold, phosphorus, exercise, *nux vomica*, hydrotherapeutic baths, rest, excitement, codeine, and aromatic spirits of ammonia. Is there anything left in the pharmacopoeia?"

"Somewhere in these mountains," said the doctor, "there's a plant growing–a flowering plant that'll cure you, and it's about the only thing that will. It's of a kind that's as old as the world; but of late it's powerful scarce and hard to find. You and I will have to hunt it up. I'm not engaged in active practice now: I'm getting along in years; but I'll take your case. You'll have to come every day in the afternoon and help me hunt for this plant till we find it. The city doctors may know a lot about new scientific things, but they don't know much about the cures that nature carries around in her saddlebags."

So every day the old doctor and I hunted the cure-all plant among the mountains and valleys of the Blue Ridge. Together we toiled up steep heights so slippery with fallen autumn leaves that we had to catch every sapling and branch within our reach to save us from falling. We waded through gorges and chasms, breast-deep with laurel and ferns; we followed the banks of mountain streams for miles; we wound our way like Indians through brakes of pine– road side, hill side, river side, mountain side we explored in our search for the miraculous plant.

As the old doctor said, it must have grown scarce and hard to find. But we followed our quest. Day by day we plumbed the valleys, scaled the heights, and tramped the plateaus in search of the miraculous plant. Mountain-bred, he never seemed to tire. I often reached home too fatigued to do anything except fall into bed and sleep until morning. This we kept up for a month.

One evening after I had returned from a six-mile tramp with the old doctor, Amaryllis and I took a little walk under the trees near the road. We looked at the mountains drawing their royal-purple robes around them for their night's repose.

"I'm glad you're well again," she said. "When you first came you frightened me. I thought you were really ill."

"Well again!" I almost shrieked. "Do you know that I have only one chance in a thousand to live?"

Amaryllis looked at me in surprise. "Why," said she, "you are as strong as one of the plough-mules, you sleep ten or twelve hours every night, and you are eating us out of house and home. What more do you want?"

"I tell you," said I, "that unless we find the magic—that is, the plant we are looking for—in time, nothing can save me. The doctor tells me so."

"What doctor?"

"Doctor Tatum—the old doctor who lives halfway up Black Oak Mountain. Do you know him?"

"I have known him since I was able to talk. And is that where you go every day—is it he who takes you on these long walks and climbs that have brought back your health and strength? God bless the old doctor."

Just then the old doctor himself drove slowly down the road in his rickety old buggy. I waved my hand at him and shouted that I would be on hand the next day at the usual time. He stopped his horse and called to Amaryllis to come out to him. They talked for five minutes while I waited. Then the old doctor drove on.

When we got to the house Amaryllis lugged out an encyclopedia and sought a word in it. "The doctor said," she told me, "that you needn't call any more as a patient, but he'd be glad to see you any time as a friend. And then he told me to look up my name in the encyclopedia and tell you what it means. It seems to be the name of a genus of flowering plants, and also the name of a country girl in Theocritus and Virgil. What do you suppose the doctor meant by that?"

"I know what he meant," said I. "I know now."

A word to a brother who may have come under the spell of the unquiet Lady Neurasthenia.

The formula was true. Even though gropingly at times, the physicians of the walled cities had put their fingers upon the specific medicament.

And so for the exercise one is referred to good Doctor Tatum on Black Oak Mountain—take the road to your right at the Methodist meeting house in the pine-grove.

Absolute rest and exercise!

What rest more remedial than to sit with Amaryllis in the shade and, with a sixth sense, read the wordless Theocritan idyl of the gold-bannered blue mountains marching orderly into the dormitories of the night?

October *and* June

he Captain gazed gloomily at his sword that hung upon the wall. In the closet nearby was stored his faded uniform, stained and worn by weather and service. What a long, long time it seemed since those old days of war's alarms!

And now, veteran that he was of his country's strenuous times, he had been reduced to abject surrender by a woman's soft eyes and smiling lips. As he sat in his quiet room, he held in his hand the letter he had just received from her—the letter that had caused him to wear that look of gloom. He re-read the fatal paragraph that had destroyed his hope:

In declining the honor you have done me in asking me to be your wife, I feel that I ought to speak frankly. The reason I have for so doing is the great difference between our ages. I like you very, very much, but I am sure that our marriage would not be a happy one. I am sorry to have to refer to this, but I believe that you will appreciate my honesty in giving you the true reason.

The Captain sighed, and leaned his head upon his hand. Yes, there were many years between their ages. But he was strong and rugged, he had position and wealth. Would not his love, his tender care, and the advantages he could bestow upon her make her forget the question of age? Besides, he was almost sure that she cared for him.

The Captain was a man of prompt action. In the field he had been distinguished for his decisiveness and energy. He would see her and plead his cause again in person. Age! – what was it to come between him and the one he loved?

In two hours he stood ready, in light marching order, for his greatest battle. He took the train for the old Southern town in Tennessee where she lived.

Theodora Deming was on the steps of the handsome, porticoed old mansion, enjoying the summer twilight, when the Captain entered the gate and came up the graveled walk. She met him with a smile that was free from embarrassment. As the Captain stood on the step below her, the difference in their ages did not appear so great. He was tall and straight and clear-eyed and browned. She was in the bloom of lovely womanhood.

"I wasn't expecting you," said Theodora; "but now that you've come you may sit on the step. Didn't you get my letter?"

"I did," said the Captain; "and that's why I came. I say, now, Theo, reconsider your answer, won't you?"

Theodora smiled softly upon him. He carried his years well. She was really fond of his strength, his wholesome looks, his manliness—perhaps, if–

"No, no," she said, shaking her head, positively; "it's out of the question. I like you a whole lot, but marrying won't do. My age and yours are—but don't make me say it again—I told you in my letter."

The Captain flushed a little through the bronze on his face. He was silent for a while, gazing sadly into the twilight. Beyond a line of woods that he could see was a field where the boys in blue had once bivouacked on their march toward the sea. How long ago it seemed now! Truly, Fate and Father Time had tricked him sorely. Just a few years interposed between himself and happiness!

Theodora's hand crept down and rested in the clasp of his firm, brown one. She felt, at least, that sentiment that is akin to love.

"Don't take it so hard, please," she said, gently. "It's all for the best. I've reasoned it out very wisely all by myself. Someday you'll be glad I didn't marry you. It would be very nice and lovely for a while–but, just think! In only a few short years what different tastes we would have! One of us would want to sit by the fireside and read, and maybe nurse neuralgia or rheumatism of evenings, while the other would be crazy for balls and theatres and late suppers. No, my dear friend. While it isn't exactly January and May, it's a clear case of October and pretty early in June."

"I'd always do what you wanted me to do, Theo. If you wanted to–"

"No, you wouldn't. You think now that you would, but you wouldn't. Please don't ask me anymore."

The Captain had lost his battle. But he was a gallant warrior, and when he rose to make his final adieu his mouth was grimly set and his shoulders were squared.

He took the train for the North that night. On the next evening he was back in his room, where his sword was hanging against the wall. He was dressing for dinner, tying his white tie into a very careful bow. And at the same time he was indulging in a pensive soliloquy.

"'Pon my honor, I believe Theo was right, after all. Nobody can deny that she's a peach, but she must be twenty-eight, at the very kindest calculation."

For you see, the Captain was only nineteen, and his sword had never been drawn except on the parade ground at Chattanooga, which was as near as he ever got to the Spanish-American War.

The Church *with an* Overshot-Wheel

akelands is not to be found in the catalogues of fashionable summer resorts. It lies on a low spur of the Cumberland range of mountains on a little tributary of the Clinch River. Lakelands proper is a contented village of two dozen houses situated on a forlorn, narrow-gauge railroad line. You wonder whether the railroad lost itself in the pine woods and ran into Lakelands from fright and loneliness, or whether Lakelands got lost and huddled itself along the railroad to wait for the cars to carry it home.

You wonder again why it was named Lakelands. There are no lakes, and the lands about are too poor to be worth mentioning.

Half a mile from the village stands the Eagle House, a big, roomy old mansion run by Josiah Rankin for the accommodation of visitors who desire the mountain air at inexpensive rates. The Eagle House is delightfully mismanaged. It is full of ancient instead of modern improvements, and it is altogether as comfortably neglected and pleasingly disarranged as your own home. But you are furnished with clean rooms and good and abundant fare: yourself and the piney woods must do the rest. Nature has provided a mineral spring, grapevine swings, and croquet—even the wickets are wooden. You have Art to thank only for the fiddle-and-guitar music twice a week at the hop in the rustic pavilion.

The patrons of the Eagle House are those who seek recreation as a necessity, as well as a pleasure. They are busy people, who may be likened to clocks that need a fortnight's winding to insure a year's running of their wheels. You will find students there from the lower towns, now and then an artist, or a geologist absorbed in construing the ancient strata of the hills. A few quiet families spend the summers there; and often one or two tired members of that patient sisterhood known to Lakelands as "schoolmarms."

A quarter of a mile from the Eagle House was what would have been described to its guests as "an object of interest" in the catalogue, had the Eagle House issued a catalogue. This was an old, old mill that was no longer a mill. In the words of Josiah Rankin, it was "the only church in the United States, sah, with an overshot-wheel; and the only mill in the world, sah, with pews and a pipe organ." The guests of the Eagle House attended the old mill church each Sabbath, and heard the preacher liken the purified Christian to bolted flour ground to usefulness between the millstones of experience and suffering. Every year about the beginning of autumn there came to the Eagle House one Abram Strong, who remained for a time an honored and beloved guest. In Lakelands he was called "Father Abram," because his hair was so white, his face so strong and kind and florid, his laugh so merry, and his black clothes and broad hat so priestly in appearance. Even new guests after three-or four-days' acquaintance gave him this familiar title.

Father Abram came a long way to Lakelands. He lived in a big, roaring town in the Northwest where he owned mills, not little mills with pews and an organ in them, but great, ugly, mountain-like mills that the freight trains crawled around all day like ants around an ant-heap. And now you must be told about Father Abram and the mill that was a church, for their stories run together.

In the days when the church was a mill, Mr. Strong was the miller. There was no jollier, dustier, busier, happier miller in all the land than he. He lived in a little cottage across the road from the mill. His hand was heavy, but his toll was light, and the mountaineers brought their grain to him across many weary miles of rocky roads.

The delight of the miller's life was his little daughter, Aglaia. That was a brave name, truly, for a flaxen-haired toddler; but the mountaineers love sonorous and stately names. The mother had encountered it somewhere in a book, and the deed was done. In her babyhood Aglaia herself repudiated the name, as far as common use went, and persisted in calling herself "Dums." The miller and his wife often tried to coax from Aglaia the source of this mysterious name, but without results. At last they arrived at a theory. In the little garden behind the cottage was a bed of rhododendrons in which the child took a peculiar delight and interest. It may have been that she perceived in "Dums" a kinship to the formidable name of her favorite flowers.

When Aglaia was four years old she and her father used to go through a little performance in the mill every afternoon, that never failed to come off, the weather permitting. When supper was ready her mother would brush her hair and put on a clean apron and send her across to the mill to bring her father home. When the miller saw her coming in the mill door he would come forward, all white with the flour dust, and wave his hand and sing an old miller's song that was familiar in those parts and ran something like this:

> "The wheel goes round,
> The grist is ground,
> The dusty miller's merry.
> He sings all day,
> His work is play,
> While thinking of his dearie."

Then Aglaia would run to him laughing, and call:

"Da-da, come take Dums home;" and the miller would swing her to his shoulder and march over to supper, singing the miller's song. Every evening this would take place.

One day, only a week after her fourth birthday, Aglaia disappeared. When last seen she was plucking wild flowers by the side of the road in front of the cottage. A little while later her mother went out to see that she did not stray too far away, and she was already gone.

Of course every effort was made to find her. The neighbors gathered and searched the woods and the mountains for miles around. They dragged every foot of the millrace and the creek for a long distance below the dam. Never a trace of her did they find. A night or two before there had been a family of wanderers camped in a grove nearby. It was conjectured that they might have stolen the child; but when their wagon was overtaken and searched she could not be found.

The miller remained at the mill for nearly two years; and then his hope of finding her died out. He and his wife moved to the Northwest. In a few years he was the owner of a modern mill in one of the important milling cities in that region. Mrs. Strong never recovered from the shock caused by the loss of Aglaia, and two years after they moved away the miller was left to bear his sorrow alone.

When Abram Strong became prosperous, he paid a visit to Lakelands and the old mill. The scene was a sad one for him, but he was a strong man, and always appeared cheery and kindly. It was then that he was inspired to convert the old mill into a church. Lakelands was too poor to build one; and the still poorer mountaineers could not assist. There was no place of worship nearer than twenty miles.

The miller altered the appearance of the mill as little as possible. The big overshot-wheel was left in its place. The young people who came to the church used to cut their initials in its soft and slowly decaying wood. The dam was partly destroyed, and the clear mountain stream rippled unchecked down its rocky bed. Inside the mill the changes were greater. The shafts and millstones and belts and pulleys were, of course, all removed. There were two rows of benches with aisles between, and a little raised platform and pulpit at one end. On three sides overhead was a gallery containing seats, and reached by a stairway inside. There was also an organ—a real pipe organ—in the gallery, that was the pride of the congregation of the Old Mill Church. Miss Phoebe Summers was the organist. The Lakelands boys proudly took turns at pumping it for her at each Sunday's service. The Rev. Mr. Banbridge was the preacher, and rode down from Squirrel Gap on his old white horse without ever missing a service. And Abram Strong paid for everything. He paid the preacher five hundred dollars a year; and Miss Phoebe two hundred dollars.

Thus, in memory of Aglaia, the old mill was converted into a blessing for the community in which she had once lived. It seemed that the brief life of the child had brought about more good than the three score years and ten of many. But Abram Strong set up yet another monument to her memory.

Out from his mills in the Northwest came the "Aglaia" flour, made from the hardest and finest wheat that could be raised. The country soon found out that the "Aglaia" flour had two prices. One was the highest market price, and the other was— nothing.

Wherever there happened a calamity that left people destitute—a fire, a flood, a tornado, a strike, or a famine, there would go hurrying a generous consignment of the "Aglaia" at its "nothing" price. It was given away cautiously and judiciously, but it was freely given, and not a penny could the hungry ones pay for it. There got to be a saying that whenever there was a disastrous fire in the poor districts of a city the fire chief's buggy reached the scene first, next the "Aglaia" flour wagon, and then the fire engines.

So this was Abram Strong's other monument to Aglaia. Perhaps to a poet the theme may seem too utilitarian for beauty; but to some the fancy will seem sweet and fine that the pure, white, virgin flour, flying on its mission of love and charity, might be likened to the spirit of the lost child whose memory it signalized.

There came a year that brought hard times to the Cumberlands. Grain crops everywhere were light, and there were no local crops at all. Mountain floods had done much damage to property. Even game in the woods was so scarce that the hunters brought hardly enough home to keep their folk alive. Especially about Lakelands was the rigor felt.

As soon as Abram Strong heard of this his messages flew; and the little narrow-gauge cars began to unload "Aglaia" flour there. The miller's orders were to store the flour in the gallery of the Old Mill Church; and that everyone who attended the church was to carry home a sack of it.

Two weeks after that Abram Strong came for his yearly visit to the Eagle House, and became "Father Abram" again.

That season the Eagle House had fewer guests than usual. Among them was Rose Chester. Miss Chester came to Lakelands from Atlanta, where she worked in a department store. This was the first vacation outing of her life. The wife of the store manager had once spent a summer at the Eagle House. She had taken a fancy to Rose, and had persuaded her to go there for her three weeks' holiday. The manager's wife gave her a letter to Mrs. Rankin, who gladly received her in her own charge and care.

Miss Chester was not very strong. She was about twenty, and pale and delicate from an indoor life. But one week of Lakelands gave her a brightness and spirit that changed her wonderfully. The time was early September when the Cumberlands are at their greatest beauty. The mountain foliage was growing brilliant with autumnal colors; one breathed aerial champagne, the nights were deliciously cool, causing one to snuggle cozily under the warm blankets of the Eagle House.

Father Abram and Miss Chester became great friends. The old miller learned her story from Mrs. Rankin, and his interest went out quickly to the slender lonely girl who was making her own way in the world.

The mountain country was new to Miss Chester. She had lived many years in the warm, flat town of Atlanta; and the grandeur and variety of the Cumberlands delighted her. She was determined to enjoy every moment of her stay. Her little hoard of savings had been estimated so carefully in connection with her expenses that she knew almost to a penny what her very small surplus would be when she returned to work.

Miss Chester was fortunate in gaining Father Abram for a friend and companion. He knew every road and peak and slope of the mountains near Lakelands. Through him she became acquainted with the solemn delight of the shadowy, tilted aisles of the pine forests, the dignity of the bare crags, the crystal, tonic mornings, the dreamy, golden afternoons full of mysterious sadness. So her health improved, and her spirits grew light. She had a laugh as genial and hearty in its feminine way as the famous laugh of Father Abram. Both of them were natural optimists; and both knew how to present a serene and cheerful face to the world.

One day Miss Chester learned from one of the guests the history of Father Abram's lost child. Quickly she hurried away and found the miller seated on his favorite rustic bench near the chalybeate spring. He was surprised when his little friend slipped her hand into his, and looked at him with tears in her eyes.

"Oh, Father Abram," she said, "I'm so sorry! I didn't know until today about your little daughter. You will find her yet some day– Oh, I hope you will."

The miller looked down at her with his strong, ready smile.

"Thank you, Miss Rose," he said, in his usual cheery tones. "But I do not expect to find Aglaia. For a few years I hoped that vagrants had stolen her, and that she still lived; but I have lost that hope. I believe that she was drowned."

"I can understand," said Miss Chester, "how the doubt must have made it so hard to bear. And yet you are so cheerful and so ready to make other people's burdens light. Good Father Abram!"

"Good Miss Rose!" mimicked the miller, smiling. "Who thinks of others more than you do?"

A whimsical mood seemed to strike Miss Chester.

"Oh, Father Abram," she cried, "wouldn't it be grand if I should prove to be your daughter? Wouldn't it be romantic? And wouldn't you like to have me for a daughter?"

"Indeed, I would," said the miller, heartily. "If Aglaia had lived I could wish for nothing better than for her to have grown up to be just such a little woman as you are. Maybe you are Aglaia," he continued, falling in with her playful mood; "can't you remember when we lived at the mill?"

Miss Chester fell swiftly into serious meditation. Her large eyes were fixed vaguely upon something in the distance. Father Abram was amused at her quick return to seriousness. She sat thus for a long time before she spoke.

"No," she said at length, with a long sigh, "I can't remember anything at all about a mill. I don't think that I ever saw a flourmill in my life until I saw your funny little church. And if I were your little girl I would remember it, wouldn't I? I'm so sorry, Father Abram."

"So am I," said Father Abram, humoring her. "But if you cannot remember that you are my little girl, Miss Rose, surely you can recollect being someone else's. You remember your own parents, of course."

"Oh, yes; I remember them very well–especially my father. He wasn't a bit like you, Father Abram. Oh, I was only making believe. Come, now, you've rested long enough. You promised to show me the pool where you can see the trout playing, this afternoon. I never saw a trout."

Late one afternoon Father Abram set out for the old mill alone. He often went to sit and think of the old days when he lived in the cottage across the road. Time had smoothed away the sharpness of his grief until he no longer found the memory of those times painful. But whenever Abram Strong sat in the melancholy September afternoons on the spot where "Dums" used to run in every day with her yellow curls flying, the smile that Lakelands always saw upon his face was not there.

The miller made his way slowly up the winding, steep road. The trees crowded so close to the edge of it that he walked in their shade, with his hat in his hand. Squirrels ran playfully upon the old rail fence at his right. Quails were calling to their young broods in the wheat stubble. The low sun sent a torrent of pale gold up the ravine that opened to the west. Early September! –it was within a few days only of the anniversary of Aglaia's disappearance.

The old overshot-wheel, half covered with mountain ivy, caught patches of the warm sunlight filtering through the trees. The cottage across the road was still standing, but it would doubtless go down before the next winter's mountain blasts. It was overrun with morning glory and wild gourd vines, and the door hung by one hinge.

Father Abram pushed open the mill door, and entered softly. And then he stood still, wondering. He heard the sound of someone within, weeping inconsolably. He looked, and saw Miss Chester sitting in a dim pew, with her head bowed upon an open letter that her hands held.

Father Abram went to her, and laid one of his strong hands firmly upon hers. She looked up, breathed his name, and tried to speak further.

"Not yet, Miss Rose," said the miller, kindly. "Don't try to talk yet. There's nothing as good for you as a nice, quiet little cry when you are feeling blue."

It seemed that the old miller, who had known so much sorrow himself, was a magician in driving it away from others. Miss Chester's sobs grew easier. Presently she took her little plain-bordered handkerchief and wiped away a drop or two that had fallen from her eyes upon Father Abram's big hand. Then she looked up and smiled through her tears. Miss Chester could always smile before her tears had dried, just as Father Abram could smile through his own grief. In that way the two were very much alike.

The miller asked her no questions; but by and by Miss Chester began to tell him.

It was the old story that always seems so big and important to the young, and that brings reminiscent smiles to their elders. Love was the theme, as may be supposed. There was a young man in Atlanta, full of all goodness and the graces, who had discovered that Miss Chester also possessed these qualities above all other people in Atlanta or anywhere else from Greenland to Patagonia. She showed Father Abram the letter over which she had been weeping. It was a manly, tender letter, a little superlative and urgent, after the style of love letters written by young men full of goodness and the graces. He proposed for Miss Chester's hand in marriage at once. Life, he said, since her departure for a three-weeks' visit, was not to be endured. He begged for an immediate answer; and if it were favorable he promised to fly, ignoring the narrow-gauge railroad, at once to Lakelands.

"And now where does the trouble come in?" asked the miller when he had read the letter.

"I cannot marry him," said Miss Chester.

"Do you want to marry him?" asked Father Abram.

"Oh, I love him," she answered, "but–" Down went her head and she sobbed again.

"Come, Miss Rose," said the miller; "you can give me your confidence. I do not question you, but I think you can trust me."

"I do trust you," said the girl. "I will tell you why I must refuse Ralph. I am nobody; I haven't even a name; the name I call myself is a lie. Ralph is a noble man. I love him with all my heart, but I can never be his."

"What talk is this?" said Father Abram. "You said that you remember your parents. Why do you say you have no name? I do not understand."

"I do remember them," said Miss Chester. "I remember them too well. My first recollections are of our life somewhere in the far South. We moved many times to different towns and states. I have picked cotton, and worked in factories, and have often gone without enough food and clothes. My mother was sometimes good to me; my father was always cruel, and beat me. I think they were both idle and unsettled.

"One night when we were living in a little town on a river near Atlanta they had a great quarrel. It was while they were abusing and taunting each other that I learned– oh, Father Abram, I learned that I didn't even have the right to be–don't you understand? I had no right even to a name; I was nobody.

"I ran away that night. I walked to Atlanta and found work. I gave myself the name of Rose Chester, and have earned my own living ever since. Now you know why I cannot marry Ralph—and, oh, I can never tell him why."

Better than any sympathy, more helpful than pity, was Father Abram's depreciation of her woes.

"Why, dear, dear! is that all?" he said. "Fie, fie! I thought something was in the way. If this perfect young man is a man at all he will not care a pinch of bran for your family tree. Dear Miss Rose, take my word for it, it is yourself he cares for. Tell him frankly, just as you have told me, and I'll warrant that he will laugh at your story, and think all the more of you for it."

"I shall never tell him," said Miss Chester, sadly. "And I shall never marry him nor anyone else. I have not the right."

But they saw a long shadow come bobbing up the sunlit road. And then came a shorter one bobbing by its side; and presently two strange figures approached the church. The long shadow was made by Miss Phoebe Summers, the organist, come to practice. Tommy Teague, aged twelve, was responsible for the shorter shadow. It was Tommy's day to pump the organ for Miss Phoebe, and his bare toes proudly spurned the dust of the road.

Miss Phoebe, in her lilac-spray chintz dress, with her accurate little curls hanging over each ear, curtsied low to Father Abram, and shook her curls ceremoniously at Miss Chester. Then she and her assistant climbed the steep stairway to the organ loft.

In the gathering shadows below, Father Abram and Miss Chester lingered. They were silent; and it is likely that they were busy with their memories. Miss Chester sat, leaning her head on her hand, with her eyes fixed far away. Father Abram stood in the next pew, looking thoughtfully out of the door at the road and the ruined cottage.

Suddenly the scene was transformed for him back almost a score of years into the past. For, as Tommy pumped away, Miss Phoebe struck a low bass note on the organ and held it to test the volume of air that it contained. The church ceased to exist, so far as Father Abram was concerned. The deep, booming vibration that shook the little frame building was no note from an organ, but the humming of the mill machinery. He felt sure that the old overshot-wheel was turning; that he was back again, a dusty, merry miller in the old mountain mill. And now evening was come, and soon would come Aglaia with flying colors, toddling across the road to take him home to supper. Father Abram's eyes were fixed upon the broken door of the cottage.

And then came another wonder. In the gallery overhead the sacks of flour were stacked in long rows. Perhaps a mouse had been at one of them; anyway the jar of the deep organ note shook down between the cracks of the gallery floor a stream of flour, covering Father Abram from head to foot with the white dust. And then the old miller stepped into the aisle, and waved his arms and began to sing the miller's song:

> "The wheel goes round,
> The grist is ground,
> The dusty miller's merry."

—and then the rest of the miracle happened. Miss Chester was leaning forward from her pew, as pale as the flour itself, her wide-open eyes staring at Father Abram like one in a waking dream. When he began the song she stretched out her arms to him; her lips moved; she called to him in dreamy tones: "Da-da, come take Dums home!"

Miss Phoebe released the low key of the organ. But her work had been well done. The note that she struck had beaten down the doors of a closed memory; and Father Abram held his lost Aglaia close in his arms.

When you visit Lakelands they will tell you more of this story. They will tell you how the lines of it were afterward traced, and the history of the miller's daughter revealed after the gipsy wanderers had stolen her on that September day, attracted by her childish beauty. But you should wait until you sit comfortably on the shaded porch of the Eagle House, and then you can have the story at your ease. It seems best that our part of it should close while Miss Phoebe's deep bass note was yet reverberating softly.

And yet, to my mind, the finest thing of it all happened while Father Abram and his daughter were walking back to the Eagle House in the long twilight, almost too glad to speak.

"Father," she said, somewhat timidly and doubtfully, "have you a great deal of money?"

"A great deal?" said the miller. "Well, that depends. There is plenty unless you want to buy the moon or something equally expensive."

"Would it cost very, very much," asked Aglaia, who had always counted her dimes so carefully, "to send a telegram to Atlanta?"

"Ah," said Father Abram, with a little sigh, "I see. You want to ask Ralph to come."

Aglaia looked up at him with a tender smile.

"I want to ask him to wait," she said. "I have just found my father, and I want it to be just we two for a while. I want to tell him he will have to wait."

New York *by* Camp Fire Light

way out in the Creek Nation we learned things about New York. We were on a hunting trip, and were camped one night on the bank of a little stream. Bud Kingsbury was our skilled hunter and guide, and it was from his lips that we had explanations of Manhattan and the queer folks that inhabit it. Bud had once spent a month in the metropolis, and a week or two at other times, and he was pleased to discourse to us of what he had seen.

Fifty yards away from our camp was pitched the teepee of a wandering family of Indians that had come up and settled there for the night. An old, old Indian woman was trying to build a fire under an iron pot hung upon three sticks.

Bud went over to her assistance, and soon had her fire going. When he came back we complimented him playfully upon his gallantry.

"Oh," said Bud, "don't mention it. It's a way I have. Whenever I see a lady trying to cook things in a pot and having trouble I always go to the rescue. I done the same thing once in a high-toned house in New York City. Heap big society teepee on Fifth Avenue. That Injun lady kind of recalled it to my mind. Yes, I endeavors to be polite and help the ladies out."

The camp demanded the particulars.

"I was manager of the Triangle B Ranch in the Panhandle," said Bud. "It was owned at that time by old man Sterling, of New York. He wanted to sell out, and he wrote for me to come on to New York and explain the ranch to the syndicate that wanted to buy. So I sends to Fort Worth and has a forty dollar suit of clothes made, and hits the trail for the big village.

"Well, when I got there, old man Sterling and his outfit certainly laid themselves out to be agreeable. We had business and pleasure so mixed up that you couldn't tell whether it was a treat or a trade half the time. We had trolley rides, and cigars, and theatre round-ups, and rubber parties."

"Rubber parties?" said a listener, inquiringly.

"Sure," said Bud. "Didn't you never attend 'em? You walk around and try to look at the tops of the skyscrapers. Well, we sold the ranch, and old man Sterling asks me 'round to his house to take grub on the night before I started back. It wasn't any high-collared affair—just me and the old man and his wife and daughter. But they was a fine-haired outfit all right, and the lilies of the field wasn't in it. They made my Fort Worth clothes carpenter look like a dealer in horse blankets and gee strings. And then the table was all pompous with flowers, and there was a whole kit of tools laid out beside everybody's plate. You'd have thought you was fixed out to burglarize a restaurant before you could get your grub. But I'd been in New York over a week then, and I was getting on to stylish ways. I kind of trailed behind and watched the others use the hardware supplies, and then I tackled the chuck with the same weapons. It ain't much trouble to travel with the high-flyers after you find out their gait. I got along fine. I was feeling cool and agreeable, and pretty soon I was talking

96

away fluent as you please, all about the ranch and the West, and telling 'em how the Indians eat grasshopper stew and snakes, and you never saw people so interested.

"But the real joy of that feast was that Miss Sterling. Just a little trick she was, not bigger than two bits' worth of chewing plug; but she had a way about her that seemed to say she was the people, and you believed it. And yet, she never put on any airs, and she smiled at me the same as if I was a millionaire while I was telling about a Creek dog feast and listened like it was news from home.

"By and by, after we had eat oysters and some watery soup and truck that never was in my repertory, a Methodist preacher brings in a kind of camp stove arrangement, all silver, on long legs, with a lamp under it.

"Miss Sterling lights up and begins to do some cooking right on the supper table. I wondered why old man Sterling didn't hire a cook, with all the money he had. Pretty soon she dished out some cheesy tasting truck that she said was rabbit, but I swear there had never been a Molly cottontail in a mile of it.

"The last thing on the program was lemonade. It was brought around in little flat glass bowls and set by your plate. I was pretty thirsty, and I picked up mine and took a big swig of it. Right there was where the little lady had made a mistake. She had put in the lemon all right, but she'd forgot the sugar. The best housekeepers slip up sometimes. I thought maybe Miss Sterling was just learning to keep house and cook–that rabbit would surely make you think so–and I says to myself, 'Little lady, sugar or no sugar I'll stand by you,' and I raises up my bowl again and drinks the last drop of the lemonade. And then all the balance of 'em picks up their bowls and does the same. And then I gives Miss Sterling the laugh proper, just to carry it off like a joke, so she wouldn't feel bad about the mistake.

"After we all went into the sitting room she sat down and talked to me quite awhile.

"'It was so kind of you, Mr. Kingsbury,' says she, 'to bring my blunder off so nicely. It was so stupid of me to forget the sugar.'

"'Never you mind,' says I, 'some lucky man will throw his rope over a mighty elegant little housekeeper someday, not far from here.'

"'If you mean me, Mr. Kingsbury,' says she, laughing out loud, 'I hope he will be as lenient with my poor housekeeping as you have been.'

"'Don't mention it,' says I. 'Anything to oblige the ladies.'"

Bud ceased his reminiscences. And then someone asked him what he considered the most striking and prominent trait of New Yorkers.

"The most visible and peculiar trait of New York folks," answered Bud, "is New York. Most of 'em has New York on the brain. They have heard of other places, such as Waco, and Paris, and Hot Springs, and London; but they don't believe in 'em. They think that town is all Merino. Now to show you how much they care for their village I'll tell you about one of 'em that strayed out as far as the Triangle B while I was working there.

"This New Yorker come out there looking for a job on the ranch. He said he was a good horseback rider, and there was pieces of tanbark hanging on his clothes yet from his riding school.

"Well, for a while they put him to keeping books in the ranch store, for he was a devil at figures. But he got tired of that, and asked for something more in the line of activity. The boys on the ranch liked him all right, but he made us tired shouting

New York all the time. Every night he'd tell us about East River and J. P. Morgan and the Eden Musee and Hetty Green and Central Park till we used to throw tin plates and branding irons at him.

"One day this chap gets on a pitching pony, and the pony kind of sidled up his back and went to eating grass while the New Yorker was coming down.

"He come down on his head on a chunk of mesquit wood, and he didn't show any designs toward getting up again. We laid him out in a tent, and he begun to look pretty dead. So Gideon Pease saddles up and burns the wind for old Doc Sleeper's residence in Dogtown, thirty miles away.

"The doctor comes over and he investigates the patient.

"'Boys,' says he, 'you might as well go to playing seven-up for his saddle and clothes, for his head's fractured and if he lives ten minutes it will be a remarkable case of longevity.'

"Of course we didn't gamble for the poor rooster's saddle–that was one of Doc's jokes. But we stood around feeling solemn, and all of us forgive him for having talked us to death about New York.

"I never saw anybody about to hand in his checks act more peaceful than this fellow. His eyes were fixed 'way up in the air, and he was using rambling words to himself all about sweet music and beautiful streets and white-robed forms, and he was smiling like dying was a pleasure.

"'He's about gone now,' said Doc. 'Whenever they begin to think they see heaven it's all off.'

"Blamed if that New York man didn't sit right up when he heard the Doc say that.

"'Say,' says he, kind of disappointed, 'was that heaven? Confound it all, I thought it was Broadway. Some of you fellows get my clothes. I'm going to get up.'

"And I'll be blamed," concluded Bud, "if he wasn't on the train with a ticket for New York in his pocket four days afterward!"

The Adventures *of* Shamrock Jolnes

am so fortunate as to count Shamrock Jolnes, the great New York detective, among my muster of friends. Jolnes is what is called the "inside man" of the city detective force. He is an expert in the use of the typewriter, and it is his duty, whenever there is a "murder mystery" to be solved, to sit at a desk telephone at headquarters and take down the messages of "cranks" who 'phone in their confessions to having committed the crime.

But on certain "off" days when confessions are coming in slowly and three or four newspapers have run to earth as many different guilty persons, Jolnes will knock about the town with me, exhibiting, to my great delight and instruction, his marvelous powers of observation and deduction.

The other day I dropped in at Headquarters and found the great detective gazing thoughtfully at a string that was tied tightly around his little finger.

"Good morning, Whatsup," he said, without turning his head. "I'm glad to notice that you've had your house fitted up with electric lights at last."

"Will you please tell me," I said, in surprise, "how you knew that? I am sure that I never mentioned the fact to any one, and the wiring was a rush order not completed until this morning."

"Nothing easier," said Jolnes, genially. "As you came in I caught the odor of the cigar you are smoking. I know an expensive cigar; and I know that not more than three men in New York can afford to smoke cigars and pay gas bills too at the present time. That was an easy one. But I am working just now on a little problem of my own."

"Why have you that string on your finger?" I asked.

"That's the problem," said Jolnes. "My wife tied that on this morning to remind me of something I was to send up to the house. Sit down, Whatsup, and excuse me for a few moments."

The distinguished detective went to a wall telephone, and stood with the receiver to his ear for probably ten minutes.

"Were you listening to a confession?" I asked, when he had returned to his chair.

"Perhaps," said Jolnes, with a smile, "it might be called something of the sort. To be frank with you, Whatsup, I've cut out the dope. I've been increasing the quantity for so long that morphine doesn't have much effect on me anymore. I've got to have something more powerful. That telephone I just went to is connected with a room in the Waldorf where there's an author's reading in progress. Now, to get at the solution of this string."

After five minutes of silent pondering, Jolnes looked at me, with a smile, and nodded his head.

"Wonderful man!" I exclaimed; "already?"

"It is quite simple," he said, holding up his finger. "You see that knot? That is to prevent my forgetting. It is, therefore, a forget-me-knot. A forget-me-not is a flower. It was a sack of flour that I was to send home!"

"Beautiful!" I could not help crying out in admiration.

"Suppose we go out for a ramble," suggested Jolnes.

"There is only one case of importance on hand just now. Old man McCarty, one hundred and four years old, died from eating too many bananas. The evidence points so strongly to the Mafia that the police have surrounded the Second Avenue Katzenjammer Gambrinus Club No. 2, and the capture of the assassin is only the matter of a few hours. The detective force has not yet been called on for assistance."

Jolnes and I went out and up the street toward the corner, where we were to catch a surface car.

Half-way up the block we met Rheingelder, an acquaintance of ours, who held a City Hall position.

"Good morning, Rheingelder," said Jolnes, halting. "Nice breakfast that was you had this morning."

Always on the lookout for the detective's remarkable feats of deduction, I saw Jolnes's eye flash for an instant upon a long yellow splash on the shirt bosom and a smaller one upon the chin of Rheingelder—both undoubtedly made by the yolk of an egg.

"Oh, dot is some of your detectiveness," said Rheingelder, shaking all over with a smile. "Vell, I pet you trinks und cigars all round dot you cannot tell vot I haf eaten for breakfast."

"Done," said Jolnes. "Sausage, pumpernickel and coffee."

Rheingelder admitted the correctness of the surmise and paid the bet. When we had proceeded on our way I said to Jolnes:

"I thought you looked at the egg spilled on his chin and shirt front."

"I did," said Jolnes. "That is where I began my deduction. Rheingelder is a very economical, saving man. Yesterday eggs dropped in the market to twenty-eight cents per dozen. Today they are quoted at forty-two. Rheingelder ate eggs yesterday, and today he went back to his usual fare. A little thing like this isn't anything, Whatsup; it belongs to the primary arithmetic class."

When we boarded the streetcar, we found the seats all occupied– principally by ladies. Jolnes and I stood on the rear platform.

About the middle of the car there sat an elderly man with a short, gray beard, who looked to be the typical, well-dressed New Yorker. At successive corners other ladies climbed aboard, and soon three or four of them were standing over the man, clinging to straps and glaring meaningly at the man who occupied the coveted seat. But he resolutely retained his place.

"We New Yorkers," I remarked to Jolnes, "have about lost our manners, as far as the exercise of them in public goes."

"Perhaps so," said Jolnes, lightly; "but the man you evidently refer to happens to be a very chivalrous and courteous gentleman from Old Virginia. He is spending a few days in New York with his wife and two daughters, and he leaves for the South tonight."

"You know him, then?" I said, in amazement.

"I never saw him before we stepped on the car," declared the detective, smilingly.

"By the gold tooth of the Witch of Endor!" I cried, "if you can construe all that from his appearance you are dealing in nothing else than black art."

"The habit of observation–nothing more," said Jolnes. "If the old gentleman gets off the car before we do, I think I can demonstrate to you the accuracy of my deduction."

Three blocks farther along the gentleman rose to leave the car. Jolnes addressed him at the door:

"Pardon me, sir, but are you not Colonel Hunter, of Norfolk, Virginia?"

"No, suh," was the extremely courteous answer. "My name, suh, is Ellison–Major Winfield R. Ellison, from Fairfax County, in the same state. I know a good many people, suh, in Norfolk–the Goodriches, the Tollivers, and the Crabtrees, suh, but I never had the pleasure of meeting yo' friend, Colonel Hunter. I am happy to say, suh, that I am going back to Virginia tonight, after having spent a week in yo' city with my wife and three daughters. I shall be in Norfolk in about ten days, and if you will give me yo' name, suh, I will take pleasure in looking up Colonel Hunter and telling him that you inquired after him, suh."

"Thank you," said Jolnes; "tell him that Reynolds sent his regards, if you will be so kind."

I glanced at the great New York detective and saw that a look of intense chagrin had come upon his clear-cut features. Failure in the slightest point always galled Shamrock Jolnes.

"Did you say your three daughters?" he asked of the Virginia gentleman.

"Yes, suh, my three daughters, all as fine girls as there are in Fairfax County," was the answer.

With that Major Ellison stopped the car and began to descend the step.

Shamrock Jolnes clutched his arm.

"One moment, sir," he begged, in an urbane voice in which I alone detected the anxiety–"am I not right in believing that one of the young ladies is an adopted daughter?"

"You are, suh," admitted the major, from the ground, "but how the devil you knew it, suh, is mo' than I can tell."

"And mo' than I can tell, too," I said, as the car went on.

Jolnes was restored to his calm, observant serenity by having wrested victory from his apparent failure; so after we got off the car he invited me into a cafe, promising to reveal the process of his latest wonderful feat.

"In the first place," he began after we were comfortably seated, "I knew the gentleman was no New Yorker because he was flushed and uneasy and restless on account of the ladies that were standing, although he did not rise and give them his seat. I decided from his appearance that he was a Southerner rather than a Westerner.

"Next I began to figure out his reason for not relinquishing his seat to a lady when he evidently felt strongly, but not overpoweringly, impelled to do so. I very quickly decided upon that. I noticed that one of his eyes had received a severe jab in one corner, which was red and inflamed, and that all over his face were tiny round marks about the size of the end of an uncut lead pencil. Also upon both of his patent leather shoes were a number of deep imprints shaped like ovals cut off square at one end.

"Now, there is only one district in New York City where a man is bound to receive scars and wounds and indentations of that sort–and that is along the sidewalks of Twenty-third Street and a portion of Sixth Avenue south of there. I knew from the imprints of trampling French heels on his feet and the marks of countless jabs in the face from umbrellas and parasols carried by women in the shopping district that he had been in conflict with the Amazonian troops. And as he was a man of intelligent appearance, I knew he would not have braved such dangers unless he had been dragged thither by his own women folk. Therefore, when he got on the car his anger at the treatment he had received was sufficient to make him keep his seat in spite of his traditions of Southern chivalry."

"That is all very well," I said, "but why did you insist upon daughters–and especially two daughters? Why couldn't a wife alone have taken him shopping?"

"There had to be daughters," said Jolnes, calmly. "If he had only a wife, and she near his own age, he could have bluffed her into going alone. If he had a young wife she would prefer to go alone. So there you are."

"I'll admit that," I said; "but, now, why two daughters? And how, in the name of all the prophets, did you guess that one was adopted when he told you he had three?"

"Don't say guess," said Jolnes, with a touch of pride in his air; "there is no such word in the lexicon of ratiocination. In Major Ellison's buttonhole there was a carnation and a rosebud backed by a geranium leaf. No woman ever combined a carnation and a rosebud into a boutonniere. Close your eyes, Whatsup, and give the logic of your imagination a chance. Cannot you see the lovely Adele fastening the carnation to the lapel so that papa may be gay upon the street? And then the romping Edith May dancing up with sisterly jealousy to add her rosebud to the adornment?"

"And then," I cried, beginning to feel enthusiasm, "when he declared that he had three daughters–"

"I could see," said Jolnes, "one in the background who added no flower; and I knew that she must be–"

"Adopted!" I broke in. "I give you every credit; but how did you know he was leaving for the South tonight?"

"In his breast pocket," said the great detective, "something large and oval made a protuberance. Good liquor is scarce on trains, and it is a long journey from New York to Fairfax County."

"Again, I must bow to you," I said. "And tell me this, so that my last shred of doubt will be cleared away; why did you decide that he was from Virginia?"

"It was very faint, I admit," answered Shamrock Jolnes, "but no trained observer could have failed to detect the odor of mint in the car."

The Lady Higher Up

ew York City, they said, was deserted; and that accounted, doubtless, for the sounds carrying so far in the tranquil summer air. The breeze was south-by-southwest; the hour was midnight; the theme was a bit of feminine gossip by wireless mythology. Three hundred and sixty-five feet above the heated asphalt the tiptoeing symbolic deity on Manhattan pointed her vacillating arrow straight, for the time, in the direction of her exalted sister on Liberty Island. The lights of the great Garden were out; the benches in the Square were filled with sleepers in postures so strange that beside them the writhing figures in Dore's illustrations of the Inferno would have straightened into tailor's dummies. The statue of Diana on the tower of the Garden–its constancy shown by its weathercock ways, its innocence by the coating of gold that it has acquired, its devotion to style by its single, graceful flying scarf, its candor and artlessness by its habit of ever drawing the long bow, its metropolitanism by its posture of swift flight to catch a Harlem train– remained poised with its arrow pointed across the upper bay. Had that arrow sped truly and horizontally it would have passed fifty feet above the head of the heroic matron whose duty it is to offer a cast-ironical welcome to the oppressed of other lands.

Seaward this lady gazed, and the furrows between steamship lines began to cut steerage rates. The translators, too, have put an extra burden upon her. "Liberty Lighting the World" (as her creator christened her) would have had a no more responsible duty, except for the size of it, than that of an electrician or a Standard Oil magnate. But to "enlighten" the world (as our learned civic guardians "Englished" it) requires abler qualities. And so poor Liberty, instead of having a sinecure as a mere illuminator, must be converted into a Chautauqua school ma'am, with the oceans for her field instead of the placid, classic lake. With a fireless torch and an empty head must she dispel the shadows of the world and teach it its A, B, C's.

"Ah, there, Mrs. Liberty!" called a clear, rollicking soprano voice through the still, midnight air.

"Is that you, Miss Diana? Excuse my not turning my head. I'm not as flighty and whirly-whirly as some. And 'tis so hoarse I am I can hardly talk on account of the peanut-hulls left on the stairs in me throat by that last boatload of tourists from Marietta, Ohio. 'Tis after being a fine evening, miss."

"If you don't mind my asking," came the bell-like tones of the golden statue, "I'd like to know where you got that City Hall brogue. I didn't know that Liberty was necessarily Irish."

"If ye'd studied the history of art in its foreign complications ye'd not need to ask," replied the offshore statue. "If ye wasn't so light-headed and giddy ye'd know that I was made by a Dago and presented to the American people on behalf of the French Government for the purpose of welcomin' Irish immigrants into the Dutch city of New York. 'Tis that I've been doing night and day since I was erected. Ye must know, Miss Diana, that 'tis with statues the same as with people–'tis not their

103

makers nor the purposes for which they were created that influence the operations of their tongues at all– it's the associations with which they become associated, I'm telling ye."

"You're dead right," agreed Diana. "I notice it on myself. If any of the old guys from Olympus were to come along and hand me any hot air in the ancient Greek I couldn't tell it from a conversation between a Coney Island car conductor and a five-cent fare."

"I'm right glad ye've made up your mind to be sociable, Miss Diana," said Mrs. Liberty. "'Tis a lonesome life I have down here. Is there anything doin' up in the city, Miss Diana, dear?"

"Oh, la, la, la!–no," said Diana. "Notice that 'la, la, la,' Aunt Liberty? Got that from 'Paris by Night' on the roof garden under me. You'll hear that 'la, la, la' at the Cafe McCann now, along with 'garsong.' The bohemian crowd there have become tired of 'garsong' since O'Rafferty, the head waiter, punched three of them for calling him it. Oh, no; the town's strickly on the bum these nights. Everybody's away. Saw a downtown merchant on a roof garden this evening with his stenographer. Show was so dull he went to sleep. A waiter biting on a dime tip to see if it was good half woke him up. He looks around and sees his little pothooks perpetrator. 'H'm!' says he, 'will you take a letter, Miss De St. Montmorency?' 'Sure, in a minute,' says she, 'if you'll make it an X.'

"That was the best thing happened on the roof. So you see how dull it is. La, la, la!"

"'Tis fine ye have it up there in society, Miss Diana. Ye have the cat show and the horse show and the military tournaments where the privates look grand as generals and the generals try to look grand as floorwalkers. And ye have the Sportsmen's Show, where the girl that measures 36, 19, 45 cooks breakfast food in a birch-bark wigwam on the banks of the Grand Canal of Venice conducted by one of the Vanderbilts, Bernard McFadden, and the Reverends Dowie and Duss. And ye have the French ball, where the original Cohens and the Robert Emmet-Sangerbund Society dance the Highland fling one with another. And ye have the grand O'Ryan ball, which is the most beautiful pageant in the world, where the French students vie with the Tyrolean warblers in doin' the cakewalk. Ye have the best job for a statue in the whole town, Miss Diana."

"'Tis weary work," sighed the island statue, "disseminatin' the science of liberty in New York Bay. Sometimes when I take a peep down at Ellis Island and see the gang of immigrants I'm supposed to light up, 'tis tempted I am to blow out the gas and let the coroner write out their naturalization papers."

"Say, it's a shame, ain't it, to give you the worst end of it?" came the sympathetic antiphony of the steeplechase goddess. "It must be awfully lonesome down there with so much water around you. I don't see how you ever keep your hair in curl. And that Mother Hubbard you are wearing went out ten years ago. I think those sculptor guys ought to be held for damages for putting iron or marble clothes on a lady. That's where Mr. St. Gaudens was wise. I'm always a little ahead of the styles; but they're coming my way pretty fast. Excuse my back a moment–I caught a puff of wind from the north– shouldn't wonder if things had loosened up in Esopus. There, now! it's in the West–I should think that gold plank would have calmed the air out in that direction. What were you saying, Mrs. Liberty?"

"A fine chat I've had with ye, Miss Diana, ma'am, but I see one of them European steamers a-sailin' up the Narrows, and I must be attendin' to me duties. 'Tis me job to extend aloft the torch of Liberty to welcome all them that survive the kicks that the steerage stewards give 'em while landin.' Sure 'tis a great country ye can come to for $8.50, and the doctor waitin' to send ye back home free if he sees yer eyes red from cryin' for it."

The golden statue veered in the changing breeze, menacing many points on the horizon with its aureate arrow.

"So long, Aunt Liberty," sweetly called Diana of the Tower. "Some night, when the wind's right. I'll call you up again. But–say! you haven't got such a fierce kick coming about your job. I've kept a pretty good watch on the island of Manhattan since I've been up here. That's a pretty sick-looking bunch of liberty chasers they dump down at your end of it; but they don't all stay that way. Every little while up here I see guys signing checks and voting the right ticket, and encouraging the arts and taking a bath every morning, that was shoved ashore by a dock laborer born in the United States who never earned over forty dollars a month. Don't run down your job, Aunt Liberty; you're all right, all right."

The Greater Coney

ext Sunday," said Dennis Carnahan, "I'll be after going down to see the new Coney Island that's risen like a phoenix bird from the ashes of the old resort. I'm going with Norah Flynn, and we'll fall victims to all the dry goods deceptions, from the red-flannel eruption of Mount Vesuvius to the pink silk ribbons on the race-suicide problems in the incubator kiosk.

"Was I there before? I was. I was there last Tuesday. Did I see the sights? I did not.

"Last Monday I amalgamated myself with the Bricklayers' Union, and in accordance with the rules I was ordered to quit work the same day on account of a sympathy strike with the Lady Salmon Canners' Lodge No.2, of Tacoma, Washington.

"'Twas disturbed I was in mind and proclivities by losing me job, bein' already harassed in me soul on account of havin' quarreled with Norah Flynn a week before by reason of hard words spoken at the Dairymen and Street-Sprinkler Drivers' semi-annual ball, caused by jealousy and prickly heat and that divil, Andy Coghlin.

"So, I says, it will be Coney for Tuesday; and if the chutes and the short change and the green-corn silk between the teeth don't create diversions and get me feeling better, then I don't know at all.

"Ye will have heard that Coney has received moral reconstruction. The old Bowery, where they used to take your tintype by force and give ye knockout drops before having your palm read, is now called the Wall Street of the island. The wienerwurst stands are required by law to keep a news ticker in 'em; and the doughnuts are examined every four years by a retired steamboat inspector. The nigger man's head that was used by the old patrons to throw baseballs at is now illegal; and, by order of the Police Commissioner the image of a man drivin' an automobile has been substituted. I hear that the old immoral amusements have been suppressed. People who used to go down from New York to sit in the sand and dabble in the surf now give up their quarters to squeeze through turnstiles and see imitations of city fires and floods painted on canvas. The reprehensible and degradin' resorts that disgraced old Coney are said to be wiped out. The wipin'-out process consists of raisin' the price from 10 cents to 25 cents, and hirin' a blonde named Maudie to sell tickets instead of Micky, the Bowery Bite. That's what they say—I don't know.

"But to Coney I goes a-Tuesday. I gets off the 'L' and starts for the glitterin' show. 'Twas a fine sight. The Babylonian towers and the Hindoo roof gardens was blazin' with thousands of electric lights, and the streets was thick with people. 'Tis a true thing they say that Coney levels all rank. I see millionaires eatin' popcorn and trampin' along with the crowd; and I see eight-dollar-a-week clothin'-store clerks in red automobiles fightin' one another for who'd squeeze the horn when they come to a corner.

"'I made a mistake,' I says to myself. 'Twas not Coney I needed. When a man's sad 'tis not scenes of hilarity he wants. 'Twould be far better for him to meditate in a graveyard or to attend services at the Paradise Roof Gardens. 'Tis no consolation when a man's lost his sweetheart to order hot corn and have the waiter bring him the powdered sugar cruet instead of salt and then conceal himself, or to have Zozookum, the gipsy palmist, tell him that he has three children and to look out for another serious calamity; price twenty-five cents.

"I walked far away down on the beach, to the ruins of an old pavilion near one corner of this new private park, Dreamland. A year ago that old pavilion was standin' up straight and the old-style waiters was slammin' a week's supply of clam chowder down in front of you for a nickel and callin' you 'cully' friendly, and vice was rampant, and you got back to New York with enough change to take a car at the bridge. Now they tell me that they serve Welsh rabbits on Surf Avenue, and you get the right change back in the movin'-picture joints.

"I sat down at one side of the old pavilion and looked at the surf spreadin' itself on the beach, and thought about the time me and Norah Flynn sat on that spot last summer. 'Twas before reform struck the island; and we was happy. We had tintypes and chowder in the ribald dives, and the Egyptian Sorceress of the Nile told Norah out of her hand, while I was waitin' in the door, that 'twould be the luck of her to marry a red-headed gossoon with two crooked legs, and I was overrunnin' with joy on account of the allusion. And 'twas there that Norah Flynn put her two hands in mine a year before and we talked of flats and the things she could cook and the love business that goes with such episodes. And that was Coney as we loved it, and as the hand of Satan was upon it, friendly and noisy and your money's worth, with no fence around the ocean and not too many electric lights to show the sleeve of a black serge coat against a white shirtwaist.

"I sat with my back to the parks where they had the moon and the dreams and the steeples corralled, and longed for the old Coney. There wasn't many people on the beach. Lots of them was feedin' pennies into the slot machines to see the 'Interrupted Courtship' in the movin' pictures; and a good many was takin' the sea air in the Canals of Venice and some was breathin' the smoke of the sea battle by actual warships in a tank filled with real water. A few was down on the sands enjoyin' the moonlight and the water. And the heart of me was heavy for the new morals of the old island, while the bands behind me played and the sea pounded on the bass drum in front.

"And directly I got up and walked along the old pavilion, and there on the other side of, half in the dark, was a slip of a girl sittin' on the tumble-down timbers, and unless I'm a liar she was cryin' by herself there, all alone.

"'Is it trouble you are in, now, Miss,' says I; 'and what's to be done about it?'

"''Tis none of your business at all, Denny Carnahan,' says she, sittin' up straight. And it was the voice of no other than Norah Flynn.

"'Then it's not,' says I, 'and we're after having a pleasant evening, Miss Flynn. Have ye seen the sights of this new Coney Island, then? I presume ye have come here for that purpose,' says I.

"'I have,' says she. 'Me mother and Uncle Tim they are waiting beyond. 'Tis an elegant evening I've had. I've seen all the attractions that be.'

"'Right ye are,' says I to Norah; and I don't know when I've been that amused. After disportin' me-self among the most laughable moral improvements of the revised shell games I took meself to the shore for the benefit of the cool air. 'And did ye observe the Durbar, Miss Flynn?'

"'I did,' says she, reflectin'; 'but 'tis not safe, I'm thinkin', to ride down them slantin' things into the water.'

"'How did ye fancy the shoot the chutes?' I asks.

"'True, then, I'm afraid of guns,' says Norah. 'They make such noise in my ears. But Uncle Tim, he shot them, he did, and won cigars. 'Tis a fine time we had this day, Mr. Carnahan.'

"'I'm glad you've enjoyed yerself,' I says. 'I suppose you've had a roarin' fine time seein' the sights. And how did the incubators and the helter-skelter and the midgets suit the taste of ye?'

"'I—I wasn't hungry,' says Norah, faint. 'But mother ate a quantity of all of 'em. I'm that pleased with the fine things in the new Coney Island,' says she, 'that it's the happiest day I've seen in a long time, at all.'

"'Did you see Venice?' says I.

"'We did,' says she. 'She was a beauty. She was all dressed in red, she was, with—'

"I listened no more to Norah Flynn. I stepped up and I gathered her in my arms.

"''Tis a story-teller ye are, Norah Flynn', says I. 'Ye've seen no more of the greater Coney Island than I have meself. Come, now, tell the truth—ye came to sit by the old pavilion by the waves where you sat last summer and made Dennis Carnahan a happy man. Speak up, and tell the truth.'

"Norah stuck her nose against me vest.

"'I despise it, Denny,' she says, half cryin'. 'Mother and Uncle Tim went to see the shows, but I came down here to think of you. I couldn't bear the lights and the crowd. Are you forgivin' me, Denny, for the words we had?'

"''Twas me fault,' says I. 'I came here for the same reason meself. Look at the lights, Norah,' I says, turning my back to the sea—'ain't they pretty?'

"'They are,' says Norah, with her eyes shinin'; 'and do ye hear the bands playin'? Oh, Denny, I think I'd like to see it all.'

"'The old Coney is gone, darlin',' I says to her. 'Everything moves. When a man's glad it's not scenes of sadness he wants. 'Tis a greater Coney we have here, but we couldn't see it till we got in the humor for it. Next Sunday, Norah darlin', we'll see the new place from end to end."

Law *and* Order

found myself in Texas recently, revisiting old places and vistas. At a sheep ranch where I had sojourned many years ago, I stopped for a week. And, as all visitors do, I heartily plunged into the business at hand, which happened to be that of dipping the sheep.

Now, this process is so different from ordinary human baptism that it deserves a word of itself. A vast iron cauldron with half the fires of Avernus beneath it is partly filled with water that soon boils furiously. Into that is cast concentrated lye, lime, and sulphur, which is allowed to stew and fume until the witches' broth is strong enough to scorch the third arm of Palladino herself.

Then this concentrated brew is mixed in a long, deep vat with cubic gallons of hot water, and the sheep are caught by their hind legs and flung into the compound. After being thoroughly ducked by means of a forked pole in the hands of a gentleman detailed for that purpose, they are allowed to clamber up an incline into a corral and dry or die, as the state of their constitutions may decree. If you ever caught an able-bodied, two-year-old mutton by the hind legs and felt the 750 volts of kicking that he can send though your arm seventeen times before you can hurl him into the vat, you will, of course, hope that he may die instead of dry.

But this is merely to explain why Bud Oakley and I gladly stretched ourselves on the bank of the nearby charco after the dipping, glad for the welcome inanition and pure contact with the earth after our muscle-racking labors. The flock was a small one, and we finished at three in the afternoon; so Bud brought from the morral[3] on his saddle horn, coffee and a coffeepot and a big hunk of bread and some side bacon. Mr. Mills, the ranch owner and my old friend, rode away to the ranch with his force of Mexican *trabajadores*.

While the bacon was frizzling nicely, there was the sound of horses' hoofs behind us. Bud's six-shooter lay in its scabbard ten feet away from his hand. He paid not the slightest heed to the approaching horseman. This attitude of a Texas ranchman was so different from the old-time custom that I marveled. Instinctively I turned to inspect the possible foe that menaced us in the rear. I saw a horseman dressed in black, who might have been a lawyer or a parson or an undertaker, trotting peaceably along the road by the *arroyo*.

Bud noticed my precautionary movement and smiled sarcastically and sorrowfully.

"You've been away too long," said he. "You don't need to look around anymore when anybody gallops up behind you in this state, unless something hits you in the back; and even then it's liable to be only a bunch of tracts or a petition to sign against the trusts. I never looked at that hombre that rode by; but I'll bet a quart of sheep dip that he's some double-dyed son of a popgun out rounding up prohibition votes."

---

[3] *A fiber bag usually used as a food bag for horses -*

"Times have changed, Bud," said I, oracularly. "Law and order is the rule now in the South and the Southwest."

I caught a cold gleam from Bud's pale blue eyes.

"Not that I–" I began, hastily.

"Of course you don't," said Bud warmly. "You know better. You've lived here before. Law and order, you say? Twenty years ago we had 'em here. We only had two or three laws, such as against murder before witnesses, and being caught stealing horses, and voting the Republican ticket. But how is it now? All we get is orders; and the laws go out of the state. Them legislators set up there at Austin and don't do nothing but make laws against kerosene oil and schoolbooks being brought into the state. I reckon they was afraid some man would go home some evening after work and light up and get an education and go to work and make laws to repeal aforesaid laws. Me, I'm for the old days when law and order meant what they said. A law was a law, and a order was a order."

"But–" I began.

"I was going on," continued Bud, "while this coffee is boiling, to describe to you a case of genuine law and order that I knew of once in the times when cases was decided in the chambers of a six-shooter instead of a supreme court.

"You've heard of old Ben Kirkman, the cattle king? His ranch run from the Nueces to the Rio Grande. In them days, as you know, there was cattle barons and cattle kings. The difference was this: when a cattleman went to San Antone and bought beer for the newspaper reporters and only give them the number of cattle he actually owned; they wrote him up for a baron. When he bought 'em champagne wine and added in the amount of cattle he had stole, they called him a king.

"Luke Summers was one of his range bosses. And down to the king's ranch comes one day a bunch of these Oriental people from New York or Kansas City or thereabouts. Luke was detailed with a squad to ride about with 'em, and see that the rattlesnakes got fair warning when they was coming, and drive the deer out of their way. Among the bunch was a black-eyed girl that wore a number two shoe. That's all I noticed about her. But Luke must have seen more, for he married her one day before the caballard[4] started back, and went over on Canada Verde and set up a ranch of his own. I'm skipping over the sentimental stuff on purpose, because I never saw or wanted to see any of it. And Luke takes me along with him because we was old friends and I handled cattle to suit him.

"I'm skipping over much what followed, because I never saw or wanted to see any of it–but three years afterward there was a boy kid stumbling and blubbering around the galleries and floors of Luke's ranch. I never had no use for kids; but it seems they did. And I'm skipping over much what followed until one day out to the ranch drives in hacks and buckboards a lot of Mrs. Summers's friends from the East–a sister or so and two or three men. One looked like an uncle to somebody; and one looked like nothing; and the other one had on corkscrew pants and spoke in a tone of voice. I never liked a man who spoke in a tone of voice.

"I'm skipping over much what followed; but one afternoon when I rides up to the ranch house to get some orders about a drove of beeves that was to be shipped, I

---

[4] *A band of saddle horses; refers to the mounts owned by a ranch when they are not being ridden (cavvy) -*

hears something like a popgun go off. I waits at the hitching rack, not wishing to intrude on private affairs. In a little while Luke comes out and gives some orders to some of his Mexican hands, and they go and hitch up sundry and divers vehicles; and mighty soon out comes one of the sisters or so and some of the two or three men. But two of the two or three men carries between 'em the corkscrew man who spoke in a tone of voice, and lays him flat down in one of the wagons. And they all might have been seen wending their way away.

"'Bud,' says Luke to me, 'I want you to fix up a little and go up to San Antone with me.'

"'Let me get on my Mexican spurs,' says I, 'and I'm your company.'

"One of the sisters or so seems to have stayed at the ranch with Mrs. Summers and the kid. We rides to Encinal and catches the International, and hits San Antone in the morning. After breakfast Luke steers me straight to the office of a lawyer. They go in a room and talk and then come out.

"'Oh, there won't be any trouble, Mr. Summers,' says the lawyer. 'I'll acquaint Judge Simmons with the facts today; and the matter will be put through as promptly as possible. Law and order reigns in this state as swift and sure as any in the country.'

"'I'll wait for the decree if it won't take over half an hour,' says Luke.

"'Tut, tut,' says the lawyer man. 'Law must take its course. Come back day after tomorrow at half-past nine.'

"At that time me and Luke shows up, and the lawyer hands him a folded document. And Luke writes him out a check.

"On the sidewalk Luke holds up the paper to me and puts a finger the size of a kitchen door latch on it and says:

"'Decree of ab-so-lute divorce with cus-to-dy of the child.'

"'Skipping over much what has happened of which I know nothing,' says I, 'it looks to me like a split. Couldn't the lawyer man have made it a strike for you?'

"'Bud,' says he, in a pained style, 'that child is the one thing I have to live for. She may go; but the boy is mine!—think of it—I have cus-to-dy of the child.'

"'All right,' says I. 'If it's the law, let's abide by it. But I think,' says I, 'that Judge Simmons might have used exemplary clemency, or whatever is the legal term, in our case.'

"You see, I wasn't inveigled much into the desirableness of having infants around a ranch, except the kind that feed themselves and sell for so much on the hoof when they grow up. But Luke was struck with that sort of parental foolishness that I never could understand. All the way riding from the station back to the ranch, he kept pulling that decree out of his pocket and laying his finger on the back of it and reading off to me the sum and substance of it. 'Cus-to-dy of the child, Bud,' says he. 'Don't forget it—cus-to-dy of the child.'

"But when we hits the ranch we finds our decree of court obviated, nolle prossed, and remanded for trial. Mrs. Summers and the kid was gone. They tell us that an hour after me and Luke had started for San Antone she had a team hitched and lit out for the nearest station with her trunks and the youngster.

"Luke takes out his decree once more and reads off its emoluments.

"'It ain't possible, Bud,' says he, 'for this to be. It's contrary to law and order. It's wrote as plain as day here, "Cus-to-dy of the child."'"

"'There is what you might call a human leaning,' says I, 'toward smashing 'em both–not to mention the child.'

"'Judge Simmons,' goes on Luke, 'is a incorporated officer of the law. She can't take the boy away. He belongs to me by statutes passed and approved by the state of Texas.'

"'And he's removed from the jurisdiction of mundane mandamuses,' says I, 'by the unearthly statutes of female partiality. Let us praise the Lord and be thankful for whatever small mercies–' I begins; but I see Luke don't listen to me. Tired as he was, he calls for a fresh horse and starts back again for the station.

"He come back two weeks afterward, not saying much.

"'We can't get the trail,' says he; 'but we've done all the telegraphing that the wires'll stand, and we've got these city rangers they call detectives on the lookout. In the meantime, Bud,' says he, 'we'll round up them cows on Brush Creek, and wait for the law to take its course.'"

"And after that we never alluded to allusions, as you might say.

"Skipping over much what happened in the next twelve years, Luke was made sheriff of Mojada County. He made me his office deputy. Now, don't get in your mind no wrong apparitions of a office deputy doing sums in a book or mashing letters in a cider press. In them days his job was to watch the back windows so nobody didn't plug the sheriff in the rear while he was adding up mileage at his desk in front. And in them days I had qualifications for the job. And there was law and order in Mojada County, and schoolbooks, and all the whiskey you wanted, and the Government built its own battleships instead of collecting nickels from the school children to do it with. And, as I say, there was law and order instead of enactments and restrictions such as disfigure our umpire state today. We had our office at Bildad, the county seat, from which we emerged forth on necessary occasions to soothe whatever fracases and unrest that might occur in our jurisdiction.

"Skipping over much what happened while me and Luke was sheriff, I want to give you an idea of how the law was respected in them days. Luke was what you would call one of the most conscious men in the world. He never knew much book law, but he had the inner emoluments of justice and mercy inculcated into his system. If a respectable citizen shot a Mexican or held up a train and cleaned out the safe in the express car, and Luke ever got hold of him, he'd give the guilty party such a reprimand and a cussin' out that he'd probable never do it again. But once let somebody steal a horse (unless it was a Spanish pony), or cut a wire fence, or otherwise impair the peace and indignity of Mojada County, Luke and me would be on 'em with habeas corpuses and smokeless powder and all the modern inventions of equity and etiquette.

"We certainly had our county on a basis of lawfulness. I've known persons of Eastern classification with little spotted caps and buttoned-up shoes to get off the train at Bildad and eat sandwiches at the railroad station without being shot at or even roped and drug about by the citizens of the town.

"Luke had his own ideas of legality and justice. He was kind of training me to succeed him when he went out of office. He was always looking ahead to the time when he'd quit sheriffing. What he wanted to do was to build a yellow house with latticework under the porch and have hens scratching in the yard. The one main thing in his mind seemed to be the yard.

"'Bud,' he says to me, 'by instinct and sentiment I'm a contractor. I want to be a contractor. That's what I'll be when I get out of office.'

"'What kind of a contractor?' says I. 'It sounds like a kind of a business to me. You ain't going to haul cement or establish branches or work on a railroad, are you?'

"'You don't understand,' says Luke. 'I'm tired of space and horizons and territory and distances and things like that. What I want is reasonable contraction. I want a yard with a fence around it that you can go out and set on after supper and listen to whip-poor-wills,' says Luke.

"That's the kind of a man he was. He was home-like, although he'd had bad luck in such investments. But he never talked about them times on the ranch. It seemed like he'd forgotten about it. I wondered how, with his ideas of yards and chickens and notions of latticework, he'd seemed to have got out of his mind that kid of his that had been taken away from him, unlawful, in spite of his decree of court. But he wasn't a man you could ask about such things as he didn't refer to in his own conversation.

"I reckon he'd put all his emotions and ideas into being sheriff. I've read in books about men that was disappointed in these poetic and fine-haired and high-collared affairs with ladies renouncing truck of that kind and wrapping themselves up into some occupation like painting pictures, or herding sheep, or science, or teaching school–something to make 'em forget. Well, I guess that was the way with Luke. But, as he couldn't paint pictures, he took it out in rounding up horse thieves and in making Mojada County a safe place to sleep in if you was well armed and not afraid of requisitions or tarantulas.

"One day there passes through Bildad a bunch of these money investors from the East, and they stopped off there, Bildad being the dinner station on the I. & G. N. They was just coming back from Mexico looking after mines and such. There was five of 'em–four solid parties, with gold watch chains, that would grade up over two hundred pounds on the hoof, and one kid about seventeen or eighteen.

"This youngster had on one of them cowboy suits such as tenderfoots bring West with 'em; and you could see he was aching to wing a couple of Indians or bag a grizzly or two with the little pearl-handled gun he had buckled around his waist.

"I walked down to the depot to keep an eye on the outfit and see that they didn't locate any land or scare the cow ponies hitched in front of Murchison's store or act otherwise unseemly. Luke was away after a gang of cattle thieves down on the Frio, and I always looked after the law and order when he wasn't there.

"After dinner this boy comes out of the dining-room while the train was waiting, and prances up and down the platform ready to shoot all antelope, lions, or private citizens that might endeavor to molest or come too near him. He was a good-looking kid; only he was like all them tenderfoots–he didn't know a law-and-order town when he saw it.

"By and by along comes Pedro Johnson, the proprietor of the Crystal Palace chili-con-carne stand in Bildad. Pedro was a man who liked to amuse himself; so he kind of herd rides this youngster, laughing at him, tickled to death. I was too far away to hear, but the kid seems to mention some remarks to Pedro, and Pedro goes up and slaps him about nine feet away, and laughs harder than ever. And then the boy gets up quicker than he fell and jerks out his little pearl-handle, and – bing! bing! bing! Pedro gets it three times in special and treasured portions of his carcass. I saw the dust fly off his clothes every time the bullets hit. Sometimes them little thirty-twos cause worry at close range.

"The engine bell was ringing, and the train starting off slow. I goes up to the kid and places him under arrest, and takes away his gun. But the first thing I knew that caballard of capitalists makes a break for the train. One of 'em hesitates in front of me for a second, and kind of smiles and shoves his hand up against my chin, and I sort of laid down on the platform and took a nap. I never was afraid of guns; but I don't want any person except a barber to take liberties like that with my face again. When I woke up, the whole outfit--train, boy, and all--was gone. I asked about Pedro, and they told me the doctor said he would recover provided his wounds didn't turn out to be fatal.

"When Luke got back three days later, and I told him about it, he was mad all over.

"'Why'n't you telegraph to San Antone,' he asks, 'and have the bunch arrested there?'

"'Oh, well,' says I, 'I always did admire telegraphy; but astronomy was what I had took up just then.' That capitalist sure knew how to gesticulate with his hands.

"Luke got madder and madder. He investigates and finds in the depot a card one of the men had dropped that gives the address of some hombre called Scudder in New York City.

"'Bud,' says Luke, 'I'm going after that bunch. I'm going there and get the man or boy, as you say he was, and bring him back. I'm sheriff of Mojada County, and I shall keep law and order in its precincts while I'm able to draw a gun. And I want you to go with me. No Eastern Yankee can shoot up a respectable and well-known citizen of Bildad, 'specially with a thirty-two caliber, and escape the law. Pedro Johnson,' says Luke, 'is one of our most prominent citizens and businessmen. I'll appoint Sam Bell acting sheriff with penitentiary powers while I'm away, and you and me will take the six forty-five northbound tomorrow evening and follow up this trail.'

"'I'm your company,' says I. 'I never see this New York, but I'd like to. But, Luke,' says I, 'don't you have to have a dispensation or a habeas corpus or something from the state, when you reach out that far for rich men and malefactors?'

"'Did I have a requisition,' says Luke, 'when I went over into the Brazos bottoms and brought back Bill Grimes and two more for holding up the International? Did me and you have a search warrant or a posse comitatus when we rounded up them six Mexican cow thieves down in Hidalgo? It's my business to keep order in Mojada County.'

"'And it's my business as office deputy,' says I, 'to see that business is carried on according to law. Between us both we ought to keep things pretty well cleaned up.'

"So, the next day, Luke packs a blanket and some collars and his mileage book in a haversack, and him and me hits the breeze for New York. It was a powerful long ride. The seats in the cars was too short for six-footers like us to sleep comfortable on; and the conductor had to keep us from getting off at every town that had five-story houses in it. But we got there finally; and we seemed to see right away that he was right about it.

"'Luke,' says I, 'as office deputy and from a law standpoint, it don't look to me like this place is properly and legally in the jurisdiction of Mojada County, Texas.'

"'From the standpoint of order,' says he, 'it's amenable to answer for its sins to the properly appointed authorities from Bildad to Jerusalem.'

"'Amen,' says I. 'But let's turn our trick sudden, and ride. I don't like the looks of this place.'

"'Think of Pedro Johnson,' says Luke, 'a friend of mine and yours shot down by one of these gilded abolitionists at his very door!'

"'It was at the door of the freight depot,' says I. 'But the law will not be balked at a quibble like that.'

"We put up at one of them big hotels on Broadway. The next morning I goes down about two miles of stair steps to the bottom and hunts for Luke. It ain't no use. It looks like San Jacinto day in San Antone. There's a thousand folks milling around in a kind of a roofed-over plaza with marble pavements and trees growing right out of 'em, and I see no more chance of finding Luke than if we was hunting each other in the big pear flat down below Old Fort Ewell. But soon Luke and me runs together in one of the turns of them marble alleys.

"'It ain't no use, Bud,' says he. 'I can't find no place to eat at. I've been looking for restaurant signs and smelling for ham all over the camp. But I'm used to going hungry when I have to. Now,' says he, 'I'm going out and get a hack and ride down to the address on this Scudder card. You stay here and try to hustle some grub. But I doubt if you'll find it. I wish we'd brought along some cornmeal and bacon and beans. I'll be back when I see this Scudder, if the trail ain't wiped out.'

"So I starts foraging for breakfast. For the honor of old Mojada County I didn't want to seem green to them abolitionists, so every time I turned a corner in them marble halls I went up to the first desk or counter I see and looks around for grub. If I didn't see what I wanted I asked for something else. In about half an hour I had a dozen cigars, five story magazines, and seven or eight railroad timetables in my pockets, and never a smell of coffee or bacon to point out the trail.

"Once a lady sitting at a table and playing a game kind of like pushpin told me to go into a closet that she called Number 3. I went in and shut the door, and the blamed thing lit itself up. I set down on a stool before a shelf and waited. Thinks I, 'This is a private dining-room.' But no waiter never came. When I got to sweating good and hard, I goes out again.

"'Did you get what you wanted?' says she.

"'No, ma'am,' says I. 'Not a bite.'

"'Then there's no charge,' says she.

"'Thanky, ma'am,' says I, and I takes up the trail again.

"By and by I thinks I'll shed etiquette; and I picks up one of them boys with blue clothes and yellow buttons in front, and he leads me to what he calls the caffay breakfast room. And the first thing I lays my eyes on when I go in is that boy that had shot Pedro Johnson. He was setting all alone at a little table, hitting a egg with a spoon like he was afraid he'd break it.

"I takes the chair across the table from him; and he looks insulted and makes a move like he was going to get up.

"'Keep still, son,' says I. 'You're apprehended, arrested, and in charge of the Texas authorities. Go on and hammer that egg some more if it's the inside of it you want. Now, what did you shoot Mr. Johnson, of Bildad, for?'

"And may I ask who you are?' says he.

"'You may,' says I. 'Go ahead.'

"'I suppose you're on,' says this kid, without batting his eyes. 'But what are you eating? Here, waiter!' he calls out, raising his finger. 'Take this gentleman's order.'

"'A beefsteak,' says I, 'and some fried eggs and a can of peaches and a quart of coffee will about suffice.'

"We talk awhile about the sundries of life and then he says:

"'What are you going to do about that shooting? I had a right to shoot that man,' says he. 'He called me names that I couldn't overlook, and then he struck me. He carried a gun, too. What else could I do?'

"'We'll have to take you back to Texas,' says I.

"'I'd like to go back,' says the boy, with a kind of a grin–'if it wasn't on an occasion of this kind. It's the life I like. I've always wanted to ride and shoot and live in the open air ever since I can remember.'

"'Who was this gang of stout parties you took this trip with?' I asks.

"'My stepfather,' says he, 'and some business partners of his in some Mexican mining and land schemes.'

"'I saw you shoot Pedro Johnson,' says I, 'and I took that little popgun away from you that you did it with. And when I did so I noticed three or four little scars in a row over your right eyebrow. You've been in rookus before, haven't you?'

"'I've had these scars ever since I can remember,' says he. 'I don't know how they came there.'

"'Was you ever in Texas before?' says I.

"'Not that I remember of,' says he. 'But I thought I had when we struck the prairie country. But I guess I hadn't.'

"'Have you got a mother?' I asks.

"'She died five years ago,' says he.

"Skipping over the most of what followed–when Luke came back I turned the kid over to him. He had seen Scudder and told him what he wanted; and it seems that Scudder got active with one of these telephones as soon as he left. For in about an hour afterward there comes to our hotel some of these city rangers in everyday clothes that they call detectives, and marches the whole outfit of us to what they call a magistrate's court. They accuse Luke of attempted kidnapping, and ask him what he has to say.

"'This snipe,' says Luke to the judge, 'shot and willfully punctured with malice and forethought one of the most respected and prominent citizens of the town of Bildad, Texas, Your Honor. And in so doing laid himself liable to the penitence of law and order. And I hereby make claim and demand restitution of the State of New York City for the said alleged criminal; and I know he done it.'

"'Have you the usual and necessary requisition papers from the governor of your state?' asks the judge.

"'My usual papers,' says Luke, 'was taken away from me at the hotel by these gentlemen who represent law and order in your city. They was two Colt's .45's that I've packed for nine years; and if I don't get 'em back, there'll be more trouble. You can ask anybody in Mojada County about Luke Summers. I don't usually need any other kind of papers for what I do.'

"I see the judge looks mad, so I steps up and says:

"'Your Honor, the aforesaid defendant, Mr. Luke Summers, sheriff of Mojada County, Texas, is as fine a man as ever threw a rope or upheld the statutes and codicils of the greatest state in the Union. But he–'

"The judge hits his table with a wooden hammer and asks who I am.

"Bud Oakley,' says I. 'Office deputy of the sheriff's office of Mojada County, Texas. Representing,' says I, 'the Law. Luke Summers,' I goes on, 'represents Order. And if Your Honor will give me about ten minutes in private talk, I'll explain the whole thing to you, and show you the equitable and legal requisition papers which I carry in my pocket.'

"The judge kind of half smiles and says he will talk with me in his private room. In there I put the whole thing up to him in such language as I had, and when we goes outside, he announces the verdict that the young man is delivered into the hands of the Texas authorities; and calls the next case.

"Skipping over much of what happened on the way back, I'll tell you how the thing wound up in Bildad.

"When we got the prisoner in the sheriff's office, I says to Luke:

"'You, remember that kid of yours–that two-year old that they stole away from you when the bust-up come?'

"Luke looks black and angry. He'd never let anybody talk to him about that business, and he never mentioned it himself.

"'Toe the mark,' says I. 'Do you remember when he was toddling around on the porch and fell down on a pair of Mexican spurs and cut four little holes over his right eye? Look at the prisoner,' says I, 'look at his nose and the shape of his head and– why, you old fool, don't you know your own son?–I knew him,' says I, 'when he perforated Mr. Johnson at the depot.'

"Luke comes over to me shaking all over. I never saw him lose his nerve before.

"'Bud,' says he. 'I've never had that boy out of my mind one day or one night since he was took away. But I never let on. But can we hold him?– Can we make him stay?– I'll make the best man of him that ever put his foot in a stirrup. Wait a minute,' says he, all excited and out of his mind–'I've got some-thing here in my desk–I reckon it'll hold legal yet–I've looked at it a thousand times–"Cus-to-dy of the child,"' says Luke–'"Cus-to-dy of the child." We can hold him on that, can't we? Le'me see if I can find that decree.'

"Luke begins to tear his desk to pieces.

"'Hold on,' says I. 'You are Order and I'm Law. You needn't look for that paper, Luke. It ain't a decree any more. It's requisition papers. It's on file in that Magistrate's office in New York. I took it along when we went, because I was office deputy and knew the law.'

"'I've got him back,' says Luke. 'He's mine again. I never thought–'

"'Wait a minute,' says I. 'We've got to have law and order. You and me have got to preserve 'em both in Mojada County according to our oath and conscience. The kid shot Pedro Johnson, one of Bildad's most prominent and–'

"'Oh, hell!' says Luke. 'That don't amount to anything. That fellow was half Mexican, anyhow.'"

Transformation *of* Martin Burney

n behalf of Sir Walter's soothing plant let us look into the case of Martin Burney.

They were constructing the Speedway along the west bank of the Harlem River. The grub-boat of Dennis Corrigan, sub-contractor, was moored to a tree on the bank. Twenty-two men belonging to the little green island toiled there at the sinew-cracking labor. One among them, who wrought in the kitchen of the grub-boat was of the race of the Goths. Over them all stood the exorbitant Corrigan, harrying them like the captain of a galley crew. He paid them so little that most of the gang, work as they might, earned little more than food and tobacco; many of them were in debt to him. Corrigan boarded them all in the grub-boat, and gave them good grub, for he got it back in work.

Martin Burney was furthest behind of all. He was a little man, all muscles and hands and feet, with a gray-red, stubbly beard. He was too light for the work, which would have glutted the capacity of a steam shovel.

The work was hard. Besides that, the banks of the river were humming with mosquitoes. As a child in a dark room fixes his regard on the pale light of a comforting window, these toilers watched the sun that brought around the one hour of the day that tasted less bitter. After the sundown supper they would huddle together on the riverbank, and send the mosquitoes whining and eddying back from the malignant puffs of twenty-three reeking pipes. Thus socially banded against the foe, they wrenched out of the hour a few well-smoked drops from the cup of joy.

Each week Burney grew deeper in debt. Corrigan kept a small stock of goods on the boat, which he sold to the men at prices that brought him no loss. Burney was a good customer at the tobacco counter. One sack when he went to work in the morning and one when he came in at night, so much was his account swelled daily. Burney was something of a smoker. Yet it was not true that he ate his meals with a pipe in his mouth, which had been said of him. The little man was not discontented. He had plenty to eat, plenty of tobacco, and a tyrant to curse; so why should not he, an Irishman, be well satisfied?

One morning as he was starting with the others for work he stopped at the pine counter for his usual sack of tobacco.

"There's no more for ye," said Corrigan. "Your account's closed. Ye are a losing investment. No, not even tobaccy, my son. No more tobaccy on account. If ye want to work on and eat, do so, but the smoke of ye has all ascended. 'Tis my advice that ye hunt a new job."

"I have no tobaccy to smoke in my pipe this day, Mr. Corrigan," said Burney, not quite understanding that such a thing could happen to him.

"Earn it," said Corrigan, "and then buy it."

Burney stayed on. He knew of no other job. At first he did not realize that tobacco had got to be his father and mother, his confessor and sweetheart, and wife and child.

For three days he managed to fill his pipe from the other men's sacks, and then they shut him off, one and all. They told him, rough but friendly, that of all things in the world tobacco must be quickest forthcoming to a fellow-man desiring it, but that beyond the immediate temporary need requisition upon the store of a comrade is pressed with great danger to friendship.

Then the blackness of the pit arose and filled the heart of Burney. Sucking the corpse of his deceased dudheen, he staggered through his duties with his barrowful of stones and dirt, feeling for the first time that the curse of Adam was upon him. Other men bereft of a pleasure might have recourse to other delights, but Burney had only two comforts in life. One was his pipe, the other was an ecstatic hope that there would be no Speedways to build on the other side of Jordan.

At meal times he would let the other men go first into the grub-boat, and then he would go down on his hands and knees, groveling fiercely upon the ground where they had been sitting, trying to find some stray crumbs of tobacco. Once he sneaked down the riverbank and filled his pipe with dead willow leaves. At the first whiff of the smoke he spat in the direction of the boat and put the finest curse he knew on Corrigan—one that began with the first Corrigans born on earth and ended with the Corrigans that shall hear the trumpet of Gabriel blow. He began to hate Corrigan with all his shaking nerves and soul. Even murder occurred to him in a vague sort of way. Five days he went without the taste of tobacco—he who had smoked all day and thought the night misspent in which he had not awakened for a pipeful or two under the bedclothes.

One day a man stopped at the boat to say that there was work to be had in the Bronx Park, where a large number of laborers were required in making some improvements.

After dinner Burney walked thirty yards down the riverbank away from the maddening smell of the others' pipes. He sat down upon a stone. He was thinking he would set out for the Bronx. At least he could earn tobacco there. What if the books did say he owed Corrigan? Any man's work was worth his keep. But then he hated to go without getting even with the hard-hearted screw who had put his pipe out. Was there any way to do it?

Softly stepping among the clods came Tony, he of the race of Goths, who worked in the kitchen. He grinned at Burney's elbow, and that unhappy man, full of race animosity and holding urbanity in contempt, growled at him: "What d'ye want, ye– Dago?"

Tony also contained a grievance–and a plot. He, too, was a Corrigan hater, and had been primed to see it in others.

"How you like-a Mr. Corrigan?" he asked. "You think-a him a nice-a man?"

"To hell with 'm," he said. "May his liver turn to water, and the bones of him crack in the cold of his heart. May dog fennel grow upon his ancestors' graves, and the grandsons of his children be born without eyes. May whiskey turn to clabber in his mouth, and every time he sneezes may he blister the soles of his feet. And the smoke of his pipe—may it make his eyes water, and the drops fall on the grass that his cows eat and poison the butter that he spreads on his bread."

Though Tony remained a stranger to the beauties of this imagery, he gathered from it the conviction that it was sufficiently anti-Corrigan in its tendency. So, with the confidence of a fellow-conspirator, he sat by Burney upon the stone and unfolded his plot.

It was very simple in design. Every day after dinner it was Corrigan's habit to sleep for an hour in his bunk. At such times it was the duty of the cook and his helper, Tony, to leave the boat so that no noise might disturb the autocrat. The cook always spent this hour in walking exercise. Tony's plan was this: After Corrigan should be asleep he (Tony) and Burney would cut the mooring ropes that held the boat to the shore. Tony lacked the nerve to do the deed alone. Then the awkward boat would swing out into a swift current and surely overturn against a rock there was below.

"Come on and do it," said Burney. "If the back of ye aches from the lick he gave ye as the pit of me stomach does for the taste of a bit of smoke, we can't cut the ropes too quick."

"All a-right," said Tony. "But better wait 'bout-a ten minute more. Give-a Corrigan plenty time get good-a sleep."

They waited, sitting upon the stone. The rest of the men were at work out of sight around a bend in the road. Everything would have gone well–except, perhaps, with Corrigan, had not Tony been moved to decorate the plot with its conventional accompaniment. He was of dramatic blood, and perhaps he intuitively divined the appendage to villainous machinations as prescribed by the stage. He pulled from his shirt bosom a long, black, beautiful, venomous cigar, and handed it to Burney.

"You like-a smoke while we wait?" he asked.

Burney clutched it and snapped off the end as a terrier bites at a rat. He laid it to his lips like a long-lost sweetheart. When the smoke began to draw he gave a long, deep sigh, and the bristles of his gray-red moustache curled down over the cigar like the talons of an eagle. Slowly the red faded from the whites of his eyes. He fixed his gaze dreamily upon the hills across the river. The minutes came and went.

"'Bout time to go now," said Tony. "That damn-a Corrigan he be in the reever very quick."

Burney started out of his trance with a grunt. He turned his head and gazed with a surprised and pained severity at his accomplice. He took the cigar partly from his mouth, but sucked it back again immediately, chewed it lovingly once or twice, and spoke, in virulent puffs, from the corner of his mouth:

"What is it, ye yaller haythen? Would ye lay contrivances against the enlightened races of the earth, ye instigator of illegal crimes? Would ye seek to persuade Martin Burney into the dirty tricks of an indecent Dago? Would ye be for murderin' your benefactor, the good man that gives ye food and work? Take that, ye punkin-colored assassin!"

The torrent of Burney's indignation carried with it bodily assault. The toe of his shoe sent the would-be cutter of ropes tumbling from his seat.

Tony arose and fled. His vendetta he again relegated to the files of things that might have been. Beyond the boat he fled and away-away; he was afraid to remain.

Burney, with expanded chest, watched his late co-plotter disappear. Then he, too, departed, setting his face in the direction of the Bronx.

In his wake was a rank and pernicious trail of noisome smoke that brought peace to his heart and drove the birds from the roadside into the deepest thickets.

The Caliph *and* The Cad

urely there is no pastime more diverting than that of mingling, incognito, with persons of wealth and station. Where else but in those circles can one see life in its primitive, crude state unhampered by the conventions that bind the dwellers in a lower sphere?

There was a certain Caliph of Bagdad who was accustomed to go down among the poor and lowly for the solace obtained from the relation of their tales and histories. Is it not strange that the humble and poverty-stricken have not availed themselves of the pleasure they might glean by donning diamonds and silks and playing Caliph among the haunts of the upper world?

There was one who saw the possibilities of thus turning the tables on Haroun al Raschid. His name was Corny Brannigan, and he was a truck driver for a Canal Street importing firm. And if you read further you will learn how he turned upper Broadway into Bagdad and learned something about himself that he did not know before.

Many people would have called Corny a snob–preferably by means of a telephone. His chief interest in life, his chosen amusement, and his sole diversion after working hours, was to place himself in juxtaposition–since he could not hope to mingle–with people of fashion and means.

Every evening after Corny had put up his team and dined at a lunch-counter that made immediateness a specialty, he would clothe himself in evening raiment as correct as any you will see in the palm rooms. Then he would betake himself to that ravishing, radiant roadway devoted to Thespis, Thais, and Bacchus.

For a time he would stroll about the lobbies of the best hotels, his soul steeped in blissful content. Beautiful women, cooing like doves, but feathered like birds of Paradise, flicked him with their robes as they passed. Courtly gentlemen attended them, gallant and assiduous. And Corny's heart within him swelled like Sir Lancelot's, for the mirror spoke to him as he passed and said: "Corny, lad, there's not a guy among 'em that looks a bit the sweller than yerself. And you drivin' of a truck and them swearin' off their taxes and playin' the red in art galleries with the best in the land!"

And the mirrors spake the truth. Mr. Corny Brannigan had acquired the outward polish, if nothing more. Long and keen observation of polite society had gained for him its manner, its genteel air, and–most difficult of acquirement–its repose and ease.

Now and then in the hotels Corny had managed conversation and temporary acquaintance with substantial, if not distinguished, guests. With many of these he had exchanged cards, and the ones he received he carefully treasured for his own use later. Leaving the hotel lobbies, Corny would stroll leisurely about, lingering at the theatre entrance, dropping into the fashionable restaurants as if seeking some friend. He rarely patronized any of these places; he was no bee come to suck honey, but a butterfly flashing his wings among the flowers whose calyces held no sweets for him. His wages were not large enough to furnish him with more than the outside garb of the gentleman. To have been one of the beings he so cunningly imitated, Corny Brannigan would have given his right hand.

One night Corny had an adventure. After absorbing the delights of an hour's lounging in the principal hotels along Broadway, he passed up into the stronghold of Thespis. Cab drivers hailed him as a likely fare, to his prideful content. Languishing eyes were turned upon him as a hopeful source of lobsters and the delectable, ascendant globules of effervescence. These overtures and unconscious compliments Corny swallowed as manna, and hoped Bill, the off horse, would be less lame in the left forefoot in the morning.

Beneath a cluster of milky globes of electric light Corny paused to admire the sheen of his low-cut patent leather shoes. The building occupying the angle was a pretentious cafe. Out of this came a couple, a lady in a white, cobwebby evening gown, with a lace wrap like a wreath of mist thrown over it, and a man, tall, faultless, assured–too assured. They moved to the edge of the sidewalk and halted. Corny's eye, ever alert for "pointers" in "swell" behavior, took them in with a sidelong glance.

"The carriage is not here," said the lady. "You ordered it to wait?"

"I ordered it for nine-thirty," said the man. "It should be here now."

A familiar note in the lady's voice drew a more especial attention from Corny. It was pitched in a key well known to him. The soft electric shone upon her face. Sisters of sorrow have no quarters fixed for them. In the index to the book of breaking hearts you will find that Broadway follows very soon after the Bowery. This lady's face was sad, and her voice was attuned with it. They waited, as if for the carriage. Corny waited too, for it was out of doors, and he was never tired of accumulating and profiting by knowledge of gentlemanly conduct.

"Jack," said the lady, "don't be angry. I've done everything I could to please you this evening. Why do you act so?"

"Oh, you're an angel," said the man. "Depend upon woman to throw the blame upon a man."

"I'm not blaming you. I'm only trying to make you happy."

"You go about it in a very peculiar way."

"You have been cross with me all the evening without any cause."

"Oh, there isn't any cause except–you make me tired."

Corny took out his card case and looked over his collection. He selected one that read: "Mr. R. Lionel Whyte-Melville, Bloomsbury Square, London." This card he had inveigled from a tourist at the King Edward Hotel. Corny stepped up to the man and presented it with a correctly formal air.

"May I ask why I am selected for the honor?" asked the lady's escort.

Now, Mr. Corny Brannigan had a very wise habit of saying little during his imitations of the Caliph of Bagdad. The advice of Lord Chesterfield: "Wear a black coat and hold your tongue," he believed in without having heard. But now speech was demanded and required of him.

"No gent," said Corny, "would talk to a lady like you done. Fie upon you, Willie! Even if she happens to be your wife you ought to have more respect for your clothes than to chin her back that way. Maybe it ain't my butt-in, but it goes, anyhow–you strike me as bein' a whole lot to the wrong."

The lady's escort indulged in more elegantly expressed but fetching repartee. Corny, eschewing his truck driver's vocabulary, retorted as nearly as he could in polite phrases. Then diplomatic relations were severed; there was a brief but lively set-to with other than oral weapons, from which Corny came forth easily victor.

A carriage dashed up, driven by a tardy and solicitous coachman.

"Will you kindly open the door for me?" asked the lady. Corny assisted her to enter, and took off his hat. The escort was beginning to scramble up from the sidewalk.

"I beg your pardon, ma'am," said Corny, "if he's your man."

"He's no man of mine," said the lady. "Perhaps he–but there's no chance of his being now. Drive home, Michael. If you care to take this–with my thanks."

Three red roses were thrust out through the carriage window into Corny's hand. He took them, and the hand for an instant; and then the carriage sped away.

Corny gathered his foe's hat and began to brush the dust from his clothes.

"Come along," said Corny, taking the other man by the arm.

His late opponent was yet a little dazed by the hard knocks he had received. Corny led him carefully into a saloon three doors away.

"The drinks for us," said Corny, "me and my friend."

"You're a queer feller," said the lady's late escort–"lick a man and then want to set 'em up."

"You're my best friend," said Corny exultantly. "You don't understand? Well, listen. You just put me wise to somethin'. I been playin' gent a long time, thinkin' it was just the glad rags I had and nothin' else. Say–you're a swell, ain't you? Well, you trot in that class, I guess. I don't; but I found out one thing– I'm a gentleman, by–and I know it now. What'll you have to drink?"

The Diamond *of* Kali

he original news item concerning the diamond of the goddess Kali was handed in to the city editor. He smiled and held it for a moment above the wastebasket. Then he laid it back on his desk and said: "Try the Sunday people; they might work something out of it."

The Sunday editor glanced the item over and said: "H'm!" Afterward he sent for a reporter and expanded his comment.

"You might see General Ludlow," he said, "and make a story out of this if you can. Diamond stories are a drug; but this one is big enough to be found by a scrubwoman wrapped up in a piece of newspaper and tucked under the corner of the hall linoleum. Find out first if the General has a daughter who intends to go on the stage. If not, you can go ahead with the story. Run cuts of the Kohinoor and J. P. Morgan's collection, and work in pictures of the Kimberley mines and Barney Barnato. Fill in with a tabulated comparison of the values of diamonds, radium, and veal cutlets since the meat strike; and let it run to a half page."

On the following day the reporter turned in his story. The Sunday editor let his eye sprint along its lines. "H'm!" he said again. This time the copy went into the wastebasket with scarcely a flutter.

The reporter stiffened a little around the lips; but he was whistling softly and contentedly between his teeth when I went over to talk with him about it an hour later.

"I don't blame the 'old man'," said he, magnanimously, "for cutting it out. It did sound like funny business; but it happened exactly as I wrote it. Say, why don't you fish that story out of the w.-b. and use it? Seems to me it's as good as the tommyrot you write."

I accepted the tip, and if you read further you will learn the facts about the diamond of the goddess Kali as vouched for by one of the most reliable reporters on the staff.

Gen. Marcellus B. Ludlow lives in one of those decaying but venerated old redbrick mansions in the West Twenties. The General is a member of an old New York family that does not advertise. He is a globetrotter by birth, a gentleman by predilection, a millionaire by the mercy of Heaven, and a connoisseur of precious stones by occupation.

The reporter was admitted promptly when he made himself known at the General's residence at about eight thirty on the evening that he received the assignment. In the magnificent library he was greeted by the distinguished traveler and connoisseur, a tall, erect gentleman in the early fifties, with a nearly white moustache, and a bearing so soldierly that one perceived in him scarcely a trace of the National Guardsman. His weather-beaten countenance lit up with a charming smile of interest when the reporter made known his errand.

"Ah, you have heard of my latest find. I shall be glad to show you what I conceive to be one of the six most valuable blue diamonds in existence."

The General opened a small safe in a corner of the library and brought forth a plush-covered box. Opening this, he exposed to the reporter's bewildered gaze a huge and brilliant diamond—nearly as large as a hailstone.

"This stone," said the General, "is something more than a mere jewel. It once formed the central eye of the three-eyed goddess Kali, who is worshipped by one of the fiercest and most fanatical tribes of India. If you will arrange yourself comfortably I will give you a brief history of it for your paper."

General Ludlow brought a decanter of whiskey and glasses from a cabinet, and set a comfortable armchair for the lucky scribe.

"The Phansigars, or Thugs, of India," began the General, "are the most dangerous and dreaded of the tribes of North India. They are extremists in religion, and worship the horrid goddess Kali in the form of images. Their rites are interesting and bloody. The robbing and murdering of travelers are taught as a worthy and obligatory deed by their strange religious code. Their worship of the three-eyed goddess Kali is conducted so secretly that no traveler has ever heretofore had the honor of witnessing the ceremonies. That distinction was reserved for myself.

"While at Sakaranpur, between Delhi and Khelat, I used to explore the jungle in every direction in the hope of learning something new about these mysterious Phansigars.

"One evening at twilight I was making my way through a teakwood forest, when I came upon a deep circular depression in an open space, in the center of which was a rude stone temple. I was sure that this was one of the temples of the Thugs, so I concealed myself in the undergrowth to watch.

"When the moon rose the depression in the clearing was suddenly filled with hundreds of shadowy, swiftly gliding forms. Then a door opened in the temple, exposing a brightly illuminated image of the goddess Kali, before which a white-robed priest began a barbarous incantation, while the tribe of worshippers prostrated themselves upon the earth.

"But what interested me most was the central eye of the huge wooden idol. I could see by its flashing brilliancy that it was an immense diamond of the purest water.

"After the rites were concluded the Thugs slipped away into the forest as silently as they had come. The priest stood for a few minutes in the door of the temple enjoying the cool of the night before closing his rather warm quarters. Suddenly a dark, lithe shadow slipped down into the hollow, leaped upon the priest; and struck him down with a glittering knife. Then the murderer sprang at the image of the goddess like a cat and pried out the glowing central eye of Kali with his weapon. Straight toward me he ran with his royal prize. When he was within two paces I rose to my feet and struck him with all my force between the eyes. He rolled over senseless and the magnificent jewel fell from his hand. That is the splendid blue diamond you have just seen—a stone worthy of a monarch's crown."

"That's a corking story," said the reporter. "That decanter is exactly like the one that John W. Gates always sets out during an interview."

"Pardon me," said General Ludlow, "for forgetting hospitality in the excitement of my narrative. Help yourself."

"Here's looking at you," said the reporter.

"What I am afraid of now," said the General, lowering his voice, "is that I may be robbed of the diamond. The jewel that formed an eye of their goddess is their most sacred symbol. Somehow the tribe suspected me of having it; and members of the band have followed me half around the earth. They are the most cunning and cruel fanatics in the world, and their religious vows would compel them to assassinate the unbeliever who has desecrated their sacred treasure.

"Once in Lucknow three of their agents, disguised as servants in a hotel, endeavored to strangle me with a twisted cloth. Again, in London, two Thugs, made up as street musicians, climbed into my window at night and attacked me. They have even tracked me to this country. My life is never safe. A month ago, while I was at a hotel in the Berkshires, three of them sprang upon me from the roadside weeds. I saved myself then by my knowledge of their customs."

"How was that, General?" asked the reporter.

"There was a cow grazing nearby," said General Ludlow, "a gentle Jersey cow. I ran to her side and stood. The three Thugs ceased their attack, knelt and struck the ground thrice with their foreheads. Then, after many respectful salaams, they departed."

"Afraid the cow would hook?" asked the reporter.

"No; the cow is a sacred animal to the Phansigars. Next to their goddess they worship the cow. They have never been known to commit any deed of violence in the presence of the animal they reverence."

"It's a mighty interesting story," said the reporter. "If you don't mind I'll take another drink, and then a few notes."

"I will join you," said General Ludlow, with a courteous wave of his hand.

"If I were you," advised the reporter, "I'd take that sparkler to Texas. Get on a cow ranch there, and the Pharisees–"

"Phansigars," corrected the General.

"Oh, yes; the fancy guys would run up against a long horn every time they made a break."

General Ludlow closed the diamond case and thrust it into his bosom.

"The spies of the tribe have found me out in New York," he said, straightening his tall figure. "I'm familiar with the East Indian cast of countenance, and I know that my every movement is watched. They will undoubtedly attempt to rob and murder me here."

"Here?" exclaimed the reporter, seizing the decanter and pouring out a liberal amount of its contents.

"At any moment," said the General. "But as a soldier and a connoisseur I shall sell my life and my diamond as dearly as I can."

At this point of the reporter's story there is a certain vagueness, but it can be gathered that there was a loud crashing noise at the rear of the house they were in. General Ludlow buttoned his coat closely and sprang for the door. But the reporter clutched him firmly with one hand, while he held the decanter with the other.

"Tell me before we fly," he urged, in a voice thick with some inward turmoil, "do any of your daughters contemplate going on the stage?"

"I have no daughters–fly for your life–the Phansigars are upon us!" cried the General.

The two men dashed out of the front door of the house.

The hour was late. As their feet struck the sidewalk strange men of dark and forbidding appearance seemed to rise up out of the earth and encompass them. One with Asiatic features pressed close to the General and droned in a terrible voice:

"Buy cast clo'!"

Another, dark-whiskered and sinister, sped lithely to his side and began in a whining voice:

"Say, mister, have yer got a dime fer a poor feller what–"

They hurried on, but only into the arms of a black-eyed, dusky-browed being, who held out his hat under their noses, while a confederate of Oriental hue turned the handle of a street organ nearby.

Twenty steps farther on General Ludlow and the reporter found themselves in the midst of half a dozen villainous-looking men with high-turned coat collars and faces bristling with unshaven beards.

"Run for it!" hissed the General. "They have discovered the possessor of the diamond of the goddess Kali."

The two men took to their heels. The avengers of the goddess pursued. "Oh, Lordy!" groaned the reporter, "there isn't a cow this side of Brooklyn. We're lost!"

When near the corner they both fell over an iron object that rose from the sidewalk close to the gutter. Clinging to it desperately, they awaited their fate.

"If I only had a cow!" moaned the reporter–"or another nip from that decanter, General!"

As soon as the pursuers observed where their victims had found refuge they suddenly fell back and retreated to a considerable distance.

"They are waiting for reinforcements in order to attack us," said General Ludlow.

But the reporter emitted a ringing laugh, and hurled his hat triumphantly into the air.

"Guess again," he shouted, and leaned heavily upon the iron object. "Your old fancy guys or thugs, whatever you call 'em, are up to date. Dear General, this is a pump we've stranded upon–same as a cow in New York (hic!) see? Thas'h why the 'nfuriated smoked guys don't attack us–see? Sacred an'mal, the pump in N' York, my dear General!"

But further down in the shadows of Twenty-eighth Street the marauders were holding a parley.

"Come on, Reddy," said one. "Let's go frisk the old 'un. He's been showin' a sparkler as big as a hen egg all around Eighth Avenue for two weeks past."

"Not on your silhouette," decided Reddy. "You see 'em rallyin' round The Pump? They're friends of Bill's. Bill won't stand for nothin' of this kind in his district since he got that bid to Esopus."

This exhausts the facts concerning the Kali diamond. But it is deemed not inconsequent to close with the following brief (paid) item that appeared two days later in a morning paper.

"It is rumored that a niece of Gen. Marcellus B. Ludlow, of New York City, will appear on the stage next season.

"Her diamonds are said to be extremely valuable and of much historic interest."

The Day We Celebrate

“In the tropics” (“Hop-along” Bibb, the bird fancier, was saying to me) “the seasons, months, fortnights, week-ends, holidays, dog-days, Sundays, and yesterdays get so jumbled together in the shuffle that you never know when a year has gone by until you're in the middle of the next one.”

“Hop-along” Bibb kept his bird store on lower Fourth Avenue. He was an ex-seaman and beachcomber who made regular voyages to southern ports and imported personally conducted invoices of talking parrots and dialectic paroquets. He had a stiff knee, neck, and nerve. I had gone to him to buy a parrot to present, at Christmas, to my Aunt Joanna.

“This one,” said I, disregarding his homily on the subdivisions of time— “this one that seems all red, white, and blue—to what genus of beasts does he belong? He appeals at once to my patriotism and to my love of discord in color schemes.”

“That's a cockatoo from Ecuador,” said Bibb. “All he has been taught to say is ‘Merry Christmas.’ A seasonable bird. He's only seven dollars; and I'll bet many a human has stuck you for more money by making the same speech to you.”

And then Bibb laughed suddenly and loudly.

“That bird,” he explained, “reminds me. He's got his dates mixed. He ought to be saying *‘E pluribus unum,’* to match his feathers, instead of trying to work the Santa Claus graft. It reminds me of the time me and Liverpool Sam got our ideas of things tangled up on the coast of Costa Rica on account of the weather and other phenomena to be met with in the tropics.

“We were, as it were, stranded on that section of the Spanish main with no money to speak of and no friends that should be talked about either. We had stoked and second-cooked ourselves down there on a fruit steamer from New Orleans to try our luck, which was discharged, after we got there, for lack of evidence. There was no work suitable to our instincts; so me and Liverpool began to subsist on the red rum of the country and such fruit as we could reap where we had not sown. It was an alluvial town, called Soledad, where there was no harbor or future or recourse. Between steamers the town slept and drank rum. It only woke up when there were bananas to ship. It was like a man sleeping through dinner until the dessert.

“When me and Liverpool got so low down that the American consul wouldn't speak to us we knew we'd struck bed rock.

“We boarded with a snuff-brown lady named Chica, who kept a rum-shop and a ladies' and gents' restaurant in a street called the calle de los Forty-seven Inconsolable Saints. When our credit played out there, Liverpool, whose stomach overshadowed his sensations of noblesse oblige, married Chica. This kept us in rice and fried plantain for a month; and then Chica pounded Liverpool one morning sadly and earnestly for fifteen minutes with a casserole handed down from the Stone Age, and we knew that we had out-welcomed our liver. That night we signed an engagement with Don Jaime McSpinosa, a hybrid banana fancier of the place, to work on his fruit preserves nine miles out of town. We had to do it or be reduced to seawater and broken doses of feed and slumber.

"Now, speaking of Liverpool Sam, I don't malign or inexculpate him to you any more than I would to his face. But in my opinion, when an Englishman gets as low as he can he's got to dodge so that the dregs of other nations don't drop ballast on him out of their balloons. And if he's a Liverpool Englishman, why, firedamp is what he's got to look out for. Being a natural American, that's my personal view. But Liverpool and me had much in common. We were without decorous clothes or ways and means of existence; and, as the saying goes, misery certainly does enjoy the society of accomplices.

"Our job on old McSpinosa's plantation was chopping down banana stalks and loading the bunches of fruit on the backs of horses. Then a native dressed up in an alligator hide belt, a machete, and a pair of AA sheeting pajamas, drives 'em over to the coast and piles 'em up on the beach.

"You ever been in a banana grove? It's as solemn as a rathskeller at seven A. M. It's like being lost behind the scenes at one of these mushroom musical shows. You can't see the sky for the foliage above you; and the ground is knee deep in rotten leaves; and it's so still that you can hear the stalks growing again after you chop 'em down.

"At night me and Liverpool herded in a lot of grass huts on the edge of a lagoon with the red, yellow, and black employees of Don Jaime. There we lay fighting mosquitoes and listening to the monkeys squalling and the alligators grunting and splashing in the lagoon until daylight with only snatches of sleep between times.

"We soon lost all idea of what time of the year it was. It's just about eighty degrees there in December and June and on Fridays and at midnight and election day and any other old time. Sometimes it rains more than at others, and that's all the difference you notice. A man is liable to live along there without noticing any fugiting of tempus until someday the undertaker calls in for him just when he's beginning to think about cutting out the gang and saving up a little to invest in real estate.

"I don't know how long we worked for Don Jaime; but it was through two or three rainy spells, eight or ten haircuts, and the life of three pairs of sail-cloth trousers. All the money we earned went for rum and tobacco; but we ate, and that was something.

"All of a sudden one day me and Liverpool find the trade of committing surgical operations on banana stalks turning to aloes and quinine in our mouths. It's a seizure that often comes upon white men in Latin and geographical countries. We wanted to be addressed again in language and see the smoke of a steamer and read the real estate transfers and gents' outfitting ads in an old newspaper. Even Soledad seemed like a center of civilization to us, so that evening we put our thumbs on our nose at Don Jaime's fruit stand and shook his grass burrs off our feet.

"It was only twelve miles to Soledad, but it took me and Liverpool two days to get there. It was banana grove nearly all the way; and we got twisted time and again. It was like paging the palm room of a New York hotel for a man named Smith.

"When we saw the houses of Soledad between the trees all my disinclination toward this Liverpool Sam rose up in me. I stood him while we were two white men against the banana brindles; but now, when there were prospects of my exchanging even cuss words with an American citizen, I put him back in his proper place. And he was a sight, too, with his rum-painted nose and his red whiskers and elephant feet with leather sandals strapped to them. I suppose I looked about the same.

"'It looks to me,' says I, 'like Great Britain ought to be made to keep such gin-swilling, scurvy, unbecoming mud larks as you at home instead of sending 'em over here to degrade and taint foreign lands. We kicked you out of America once and we ought to put on rubber boots and do it again.'

"'Oh, you go to 'ell,' says Liverpool, which was about all the repartee he ever had.

"Well, Soledad, looked fine to me after Don Jaime 's plantation. Liverpool and me walked into it side by side, from force of habit, past the calabosa and the Hotel Grande, down across the plaza toward Chica's hut, where we hoped that Liverpool, being a husband of hers, might work his luck for a meal.

"As we passed the two-story little frame house occupied by the American Club, we noticed that the balcony had been decorated all around with wreaths of evergreens and flowers, and the flag was flying from the pole on the roof. Stanzey, the consul, and Arkright, a gold-mine owner, were smoking on the balcony. Me and Liverpool waved our dirty hands toward 'em and smiled real society smiles; but they turned their backs to us and went on talking. And we had played whist once with the two of 'em up to the time when Liverpool held all thirteen trumps for four hands in succession. It was some holiday, we knew; but we didn't know the day nor the year.

"A little further along we saw a reverend man named Pendergast, who had come to Soledad to build a church, standing under a cocoanut palm with his little black alpaca coat and green umbrella.

"'Boys, boys!' says he, through his blue spectacles, 'is it as bad as this? Are you so far reduced?'

"'We're reduced,' says I, 'to very vulgar fractions.'

"'It is indeed sad,' says Pendergast, 'to see my countrymen in such circumstances.'

"'Cut 'arf of that out, old party,' says Liverpool. 'Cawn't you tell a member of the British upper classes when you see one?'

"'Shut up,' I told Liverpool. 'You're on foreign soil now, or that portion of it that's not on you.'

"'And on this day, too!' goes on Pendergast, grievous–'on this most glorious day of the year when we should all be celebrating the dawn of Christian civilization and the downfall of the wicked.'

"'I did notice bunting and bouquets decorating the town, reverend,' says I, 'but I didn't know what it was for. We've been so long out of touch with calendars that we didn't know whether it was summer time or Saturday afternoon.'

"'Here is two dollars,' says Pendergast digging up two Chili silver wheels and handing 'em to me. 'Go, my men, and observe the rest of the day in a befitting manner.'

"Me and Liverpool thanked him kindly, and walked away.

"'Shall we eat?' I asks.

"'Oh, 'ell!' says Liverpool. 'What's money for?'

"'Very well, then,' I says, 'since you insist upon it, we'll drink.'

"So we pull up in a rum shop and get a quart of it and go down on the beach under a cocoanut tree and celebrate.

"Not having eaten anything but oranges in two days, the rum has immediate effect; and once more I conjure up great repugnance toward the British nation.

"'Stand up here,' I says to Liverpool, 'you scum of a despot limited monarchy, and have another dose of Bunker Hill. That good man, Mr. Pendergast,' says I, 'said we were to observe the day in a befitting manner, and I'm not going to see his money misapplied.'

"'Oh, you go to 'ell!' says Liverpool, and I started in with a fine left-hander on his right eye.

"Liverpool had been a fighter once, but dissipation and bad company had taken the nerve out of him. In ten minutes I had him lying on the sand waving the white flag.

"'Get up,' says I, kicking him in the ribs, 'and come along with me.'

"Liverpool got up and followed behind me because it was his habit, wiping the red off his face and nose. I led him to Reverend Pendergast's shack and called him out.

"'Look at this, sir,' says I–'look at this thing that was once a proud Britisher. You gave us two dollars and told us to celebrate the day. The Star-Spangled Banner still waves. Hurrah for the stars and eagles!'

"'Dear me,' says Pendergast, holding up his hands. 'Fighting on this day of all days! On Christmas day, when peace on–'

"'Christmas, hell!' says I. 'I thought it was the Fourth of July.'"

"Merry Christmas!" said the red, white, and blue cockatoo.

"Take him for six dollars," said Hop-along Bibb. "He's got his dates and colors mixed."

CPSIA information can be obtained
at www.ICGtesting.com
Printed in the USA
LVHW100419261121
704491LV00002B/45

9 781603 868211